Melilah
MANCHESTER JOURNAL
OF JEWISH STUDIES

Normative Judaism?
Jews, Judaism and
Jewish Identity

Proceedings of the British Association for
Jewish Studies (BAJS) conference 2008

Melilah
MANCHESTER JOURNAL
OF JEWISH STUDIES

Normative Judaism? Jews, Judaism and Jewish Identity

Proceedings of the British Association for
Jewish Studies (BAJS) conference 2008

Supplementary Volume No.1 (2012)

EDITORS

Daniel R. Langton and Philip S. Alexander

EDITORIAL ASSISTANT

Francesca Frazer

A publication of the Centre for Jewish Studies,
University of Manchester, United Kingdom.

Co-published by

gorgias
press

Co-Published by Gorgias Press LLC
954 River Road
Piscataway, NJ 08854
USA
Internet: www.gorgiaspress.com
Email: helpdesk@gorgiaspress.com

ISSN 1759-1953

This volume is printed on acid-free paper that meets the American National Standard for Permanence of paper for Printed Library Materials.

Printed in the United States of America

Melilah: Manchester Journal of Jewish Studies is distributed electronically free of charge at http://www.mucjs.org/MELILAH/

Melilah is an interdisciplinary journal concerned with Jewish law, history, literature, religion, culture and thought in the ancient, medieval and modern eras. It was launched in 2004 by Bernard Jackson and Ephraim Nissan under the auspices of the Centre for Jewish Studies at the University of Manchester as the New Series of the journal of the same name founded by Edward Robertson and Meir Wallenstein and published (in Hebrew) by Manchester University Press from 1944 to 1955. Five substantial volumes, each of around two hundred pages, were produced before the series was discontinued. In his editorial foreword to the first edition, Robertson explained that *Melilah* had been established to promote Jewish scholarship in the face of the threat posed by the War and its aftermath. The title of the journal refers to the ears of corn that are plucked to rub in the hands before the grains can be eaten (Deut. 23:25).

Melilah
MANCHESTER JOURNAL
OF JEWISH STUDIES

Normative Judaism?
Jews, Judaism and
Jewish Identity

CONTENTS

PREFACE

This collection of essays had its origins in the JudaicaFest conference in Manchester, UK, in 2008. This comprised end-on conferences of the British Association for Jewish Studies (on the theme 'Normative Judaism' organised by its president Philip Alexander and its secretary Daniel Langton), The Jewish Law Association (Fifteenth Biennial Conference, organised by its president Bernard Jackson) and a colloquium on Jewish Culture in the Age of Globalisation (organised by Cathy Gelbin). It is with considerable warmth and pride that my co-editor Philip Alexander and I look back upon this conference and we wish to express our profound thanks to our colleague, Bernard Jackson, the conference's primary organiser, without whom the JudaicaFest would not have been the highly productive and successful event that it turned out to be. The JLA published its proceedings as Leib Moscovitz, ed., *The Manchester Conference Volume* (Liverpool: Deborah Charles Publications, 2010; Jewish Law Association Studies XX). The Globalisation colloquium published its proceedings as Cathy Gelbin and Sander Gilman, eds., *Jewish Culture in the Age of Globalization*, European Review of History 18:01 (2011). And the BAJS conference proceedings have now been published as a supplementary volume of *Melilah: The Manchester Journal of Jewish Studies* in 2012. We would also like to express our gratitude to the journal's editorial assistant, Francesca Frazer for her assistance with proofreading.

The co-editors have collected together a selection of papers from the BAJS conference with the sincere hope that it will engender serious debate on the question of normativity in the study of Judaism and Jewish identity. The contributions, which take the form of case-studies mainly but not exclusively from the modern period, seek to address questions that relate to how and why certain aspects of Jewish life and thought come to be regarded as authoritative or normative, rather than inauthentic or marginal. No attempt has been made to synthesize or harmonize their conclusions; rather, the approach adopted is to allow the presentations from a variety of disciplines, including philosophy, musicology, history, Jewish law, and cultural studies, to speak for themselves. The case-studies include the medieval philosopher Moses Maimonides, the composer Felix Mendelssohn, the self-perception of communal leadership in Manchester during the late nineteenth-century, sermons of Anglo-Jewish Reform rabbis during the Second World War, Orthodox rabbinic debate about war in general, the idea of Jewish music, and representations of Jews in recent photographic exhibitions. The collection begins with a stout defence of normativity in the academic study of Judaism.

Daniel R. Langton and Philip S. Alexander
Centre for Jewish Studies, University of Manchester
Manchester, 2012

IN DEFENCE OF NORMATIVITY IN THE STUDY OF JUDAISM

Philip Alexander*

Normativity, as defined here in relation to Jewish religion, has two levels of meaning: firstly, the discovery and articulation of norms in relation to beliefs, practices and social structures characteristic of Judaism, and, secondly, an analytical category that facilitates the evaluation of any group that defines itself as Jewish as being marginal/central, radical/conservative, or innovative/traditional. This methodological approach is by no means essentialist. It is rather a pragmatic approach whose utility can be seen, for example, in resolving the practical challenges faced when prioritising which of a multitude of materials should be included in a university undergraduate introductory course to Judaism. It is premised on a criterion of universality: the more universal a phenomenon (in relation to Jewish self-perception and across space and time), the more it qualifies for inclusion as normative. The case of the Beta Israel and the question of their Jewish identity provides one illustration of the way in which such a methodological approach, which is fundamentally historical in character, can result in a conclusion that is at odds with many social, religious, and political claims. In the end, the problem to be faced whatever approach is adopted is whether normativity as determined by academic criteria and analysis, and normativity as determined within the faith communities, carry any implications for each other in the real world.

Preamble

I have found as I have grown older and garnered more experience in teaching and researching Jewish Studies that I have become more reflective about what I do. In particular I have become fascinated by the problem of normativity in the academic study of Judaism. Does normativity have a role to play in our discipline, and if so what should it be? So I decided to make this the theme of our conference. I started with the distinct impression that normativity is not a concept to which colleagues warm easily (after all, isn't description and explanation rather than prescription the cardinal rule of the academy?), and this is why I have given the title of my paper an apologetic ring, '*In defence of* normativity in the study of Judaism'. What I am about to argue probably goes against the grain of current thinking, against colleagues' deepest instincts, but the issues are important, and I think it is worth saying.

Normativity: a preliminary definition

When I sent out the call for papers I deliberately did not attempt to define what I meant by normativity, and I have been intrigued by how people have reacted to the term. Clearly it

* Emeritus Professor of Post-Biblical Jewish Literature, University of Manchester. Email: philip.alexander@ manchester.ac.uk The text which follows gives the substance of my Presidential Address to the British Association for Jewish Studies Annual Conference in 2008, more or less as spoken. To have elaborated on it, and exhaustively footnoted it, would have defeated its purpose, which was to spark off a discussion of the issues it raises.

means something to most. 'Normative Judaism' is an expression that has been around in Jewish Studies for decades now. I have a suspicion it may have arisen in an attempt to avoid the much more tendentious 'Orthodox Judaism' of earlier scholarship, though it doesn't seem in much favour now.[1] What, then, do *I* mean by normativity? The term for me has two levels of meaning, the one emerging from the other – the first descriptive, the second implicitly prescriptive. At the first level normativity means the discovery and articulation of norms. What I mean by a norm here is perhaps best understood on the analogy of the concept of a social norm as 'a pattern or trait taken or estimated to be typical of the behaviour of a social group because most frequently observed' (see the Mirriam-Webster Dictionary). So the norms of Judaism are the beliefs, practices and social structures that are most characteristic of Judaism. Normativity is the search for and articulation of those dominant traits. Normative Judaism is Judaism described in terms of those dominant traits. There is, of course, a problem in deciding the boundaries of Judaism. What is the entity whose dominant traits I seek? That will become clear in due course. Suffice to say here that I am happy to work initially with whatever presents itself phenomenologically to me as Judaism, though at the end of my deliberations I may want to discriminate between phenomena in terms of their conformity to or divergence from the dominant traits.

This is the descriptive level. So far, so uncontroversial, I think. But why don't I just leave it at that? Why not talk about 'common' or 'core' or 'traditional' or 'historical' Judaism'? Why use a word which carries overtones of *prescription*? The answer is that I am convinced the *description* of the norms, if validly achieved, unavoidably becomes in a certain sense *prescriptive*: it potentially allows me, as an academic, to make certain kinds of value-judgement, to pronounce, with a degree of authority, from an external perspective on the validity of claims that may be made *within* the tradition. The norms I describe are not norms in the sense of J.L. Austin's legal norms as commands from a higher authority that must be obeyed on pain of sanction,[2] though that is how some of them would be viewed within the faith communities. Rather they function more like *differentia* within a natural taxonomy – like the characteristics which allow one to classify, for example, a particular bird, as belonging to a certain genus or species. On the basis of these norms I can determine, for example, whether a given group that claims to be Jewish is, in fact, central or marginal to Judaism, or whether its beliefs or practices or social structures are radical/innovative or conservative/traditional. The description becomes an important instrument of analysis and evaluation. But this evaluation may in turn, depending on one's idea of truth, carry implications for, and even directly support or challenge, the group's own claim to be authentically Jewish. Colleagues, I know, find the blurring here of the etic/emic boundary deeply uncomfortable. It raises the spectre of the academy being sucked into the internal controversies of the faith communities it studies, or the 'purity' of its research being sullied by being exploited by religious groups for

---

[1] See the succinct account of its 'demise' in Jacob Neusner, *Studying Classical Judaism: A Primer* (Louisville, Kentucky: Westminster/John Knox Press, 1991), especially 17–36. It should be pointed out that Neusner is concerned in this volume with Judaism in the first six centuries CE (what he calls 'Classical Judaism'), rather than with Judaism over a longer time-span. The case may be somewhat different if we take the long view of Judaism down to the present day, but it is striking how he assumes that the discovery of diversity in Judaism in late antiquity *ipso facto* destroys any idea of normativity. To me this is a *non sequitur*.

[2] J.L. Austin, *The Province of Jurisprudence Determined* (London: Weidenfeld and Nicolson, 1971). My concept of a norm is closer to Hayek's idea of a norm as the outcome of a practice iterated so often and so long that it becomes a standard of behaviour (F. Hayek, *Law, Legislation and Liberty* [London: Routledge & Kegan Paul, 1969]).

polemical ends, but I would suggest that these very real fears should not be addressed simply by being denied or ignored, but by recognizing that the relationship between the academy and the faith communities it studies is a tangled one, which frustrates any straightforward objectification of religion as a field of science, and by negotiating that relationship in more subtle and mature ways.

The wrong sort of normativity: Essentialism

I shall now try to tease this out. First let me begin by making clear the sort of approach to discovering the norms of Judaism that I am *not* advocating. I reject the approach exemplified by the search for the essence of Judaism that was integral from its outset to the intellectual programme of the *Wissenschaft des Judentums*.[3] This saw Judaism as fundamentally a rational religion, and identified as central to it those elements that were in accord with reason. Strictly speaking the *wissenschaftlich* approach did not have to deny the irrational in Jewish tradition. It could have acknowledged those irrational aspects in the past, though it was vital for it to find there also enough of the rational to establish Judaism's potential to evolve, in keeping with the spirit of the age, into a religion of reason, and so take its place in the vanguard of enlightened European thought. In practice, however, the *wissenschaftlich* scholars stressed the rational heritage of Judaism – the philosophical and the ethical (and to some extent the legal) – to such an extent that they almost totally ignored everything else. If the supreme philosophical articulation of this view is Hermann Cohen's *Religion der Vernunft aus den Quellen des Judentums* (1919), its classic historical expression can be found in Heinrich Graetz's, *Geschichte der Juden* (1853–1870), and its classic creedal formulation in the Reform Movement's Pittsburgh Platform of 1885.[4] Graetz is famous in his history for his anti-mystical stance. When he comes to describe a mystical movement within Judaism – the Spanish Qabbalah, Hasidism – he can barely conceal his contempt, and he tries his hardest to show that these movements were foreign imports into Judaism, contrary to its spirit, the recrudescence of mythical ways of thinking which Judaism had long since transcended.

A strong reaction to this rationalism set in the twentieth century. One of its major champions was Gershom Scholem, who fiercely attacked the *Wissenschaft des Judentums*, and spent a life-time arguing that mysticism, far from being an alien intrusion, was central to

---

[3] See Immanuel Wolf, 'On the Concept of a Science of Judaism', in: P.R. Mendes-Flohr and Jehuda Reinharz, eds., *The Jew in the Modern World: A Documentary History* (New York: Oxford University Press, 1980), 194–95: 'The aim will be to depict Judaism, first from a historical standpoint, as it has gradually developed and taken shape, and then philosophically, according to its inner essence and idea. The textual knowledge of the literature of Judaism must precede both methods of study. Thus we have, first, the textual study of Judaism; second, a history of Judaism; third a philosophy of Judaism.' For Wolf that philosophy of Judaism will have to be based on science and reason, because that is in accord with the spirit of the times. That philosophy has yet to evolve, and it will take struggle and effort to bring it to birth, but it will nevertheless be compatible with the principle or essence of Judaism: Jews 'must raise themselves and their principle to the level of a science, for this is the attitude of the European world. On this level the relationship of strangeness in which Jews and Judaism have hitherto stood to the outside world must vanish. And if one day a bond is to join the whole of humanity, then it is *the bond of science, the bond of pure rationality, the bond of truth.*' Hermann Cohen's *Religion of Reason* (see below) and Leo Baeck's *The Essence of Judaism* (New York: Schocken Books, 1961) are classic outworkings of this programme.

[4] See Article 6: 'We recognize in Judaism a progressive religion, ever striving to be in accord with the postulates of reason.'

Judaism, and, indeed, the engine of its creativity and the basis of its survival.[5] This was, arguably, the agenda of the whole of Scholem's vast *œuvre*, but if one were to single out one work which encapsulates this thesis, then it has to be his great monograph on Shabbetai Zevi in which he attempted to argue that the seventeenth century 'false messiah', and the antinomian movement he founded, were an authentic expression of Jewish religious consciousness.[6] Scholem inspired a veritable industry of PhDs and scholarly studies, which shows no sign of abating, to recover 'lost Judaisms', and to describe Judaism from the margins – a trend which plays well to the academic fascination with the paradoxical and exotic.

But Scholem in turn came under fire for claiming too much for mysticism, and coming close to seeing it as the 'essence of Judaism'. One of his most trenchant critics was the Israeli philosopher Eli Schweid, who complained about the paradoxes that Scholem's approach engendered.[7] For Schweid there was nothing positive about Sabbatianism: it was a pathological distortion of Jewish religious consciousness which led only to tragedy and disaster. For him the essence of Judaism lies in 'the historical myth of the Jewish people' which articulates a view of Israel's relationship to God first enunciated in the biblical-prophetic narratives, but finds concrete expression in halakhah and ethics with their focus on life in the here and now, rather than on escape into some transcendent, otherworldly realm accessed by mystical praxis. Schweid defended the *Wissenschaft des Judentums* scholars against many of Scholem's strictures, and insofar as he has a marked preference for the rational, the moral and the institutional in Judaism he represents an attempt to rehabilitate their views, though his emphasis on the national is new – a consequence of his post-Zionist perspective. Nathan Rotenstreich and Joseph Dan have defended Scholem, and so the debate has rolled merrily on.[8]

A pragmatic, pedagogical approach

The essence of Judaism lies in halakhah, it lies in ethics, or in mysticism, or in philosophy – all these views have been advanced by serious thinkers. The debate is fascinating and important, but I have deep problems with it. It is far too abstract and *a priori* for my liking – much too 'Hegelian'. It may make for exciting theology, but, like much theology, I find it impossible to verify its claims and counter-claims in any meaningful way from any facts I know. I find cloudy constructs such as the 'spirit of Judaism', 'Jewish consciousness', 'the

---

[5] For a summary of Scholem's views of *Wissenschaft des Judentums* see David Biale, *Gershom Scholem: Kabbalah and Counter History* 2nd ed. (Cambridge, Mass: Harvard University Press, 1982), 1–15. Interestingly Scholem's criticism of *Wissenschaft* is as much about its de-nationalization of Judaism, as about its privileging of the rational within Jewish tradition. However, Scholem himself, in his working-methods as a scholar, was thoroughly *wissenschaftlich*, and stressed the historical, the textual, and the philological. This came out very clearly in his controversy with Martin Buber over the interpretation of Hasidism. He had no patience with Buber's more intuitive, empathetic hermeneutics – an approach that in these post-modern times would raise few eyebrows in some areas of the academy.

[6] G. Scholem, *Sabbatai Sevi: The Mystical Messiah* (Princeton: Princeton University Press, 1976).

[7] Eliezer Schweid, *Judaism and Mysticism according to Gershom Scholem: A Critical Analysis and Programmatic Discussion*, trans. David Avraham Weiner (Atlanta, Georgia: Scholars Press, 1985).

[8] See, for example, Nathan Rotenstreich, 'Symbolism and Transcendence: On Some Philosophical Aspects of Gershom Scholem's Opus', *The Review of Metaphysics* 31 (1978), 604–614; Joseph Dan, *Gershom Scholem and the Mystical Dimension of Judaism* (New York: New York University Press, 1988).

Jewish principle' practically meaningless. My intellectual formation is within a tradition of British pragmatism, far removed from the heady metaphysics of continental philosophy and theory. I prefer to work inductively – to start with concrete situations, and reflect on actual practice. The problem which I am trying to analyse here has vexed me ever since, in 1972, I put on my first course in Jewish Studies. Almost every year since then I have taught in the first year an 'Introduction to Judaism', to a class usually of around sixty students from very different backgrounds – the majority Christian, though from different wings of the Church; a small but significant proportion Jewish, though again from a wide spectrum of observance and belief; and increasingly in recent years a clutch of Muslim students, including, occasionally, women fully veiled. I have ten weeks of three hours a week in which to introduce them to Judaism. Clearly I cannot cover everything, I have to be selective, but on what basis do I make my selection? In one sense, the answer is obvious: I should choose those elements which are most central to the tradition. Faced with a choice between two topics, I should always, rationally, favour the one that is more central and set aside the one that is more peripheral. Easily enough said, but how to I distinguish centre and periphery?

Over the years I have come to discriminate on the basis of a number of very broad principles. I begin with a fundamental distinction I perceive between Judaism and *Yiddishkeit*. I feel I have to focus on the *religious* tradition, on what Jews do *religiously*, not simply on what Jews do. I have to be careful in this context not to be too restrictive in my definition of what constitutes religion. It would be seriously distorting if I were to apply to Judaism the narrow definition of religion which has dominated European thought since the Reformation, with its sharp distinction between the religious and the secular, between the Church and the State, resulting in the increasing relegation of religion to the personal and private sphere. Judaism historically is the culture of a people that embraces areas which in the west would be seen as belonging to the realm of the secular state. On the other hand I cannot widen my perspective so far as to include all the Jewish folkways relating to diet, dress, language, gesture, behaviour, which I include under the term *Yiddishkeit*. Now do not get me wrong. These folkways can be immensely important in defining Jewish identity 'on the street': in fact for outsiders, and for some Jews themselves, they *are* Jewish identity, and they are worth studying, but they do not figure much in my 'Introduction'. Why not? Because they are ephemeral, and local. And a significant proportion of those folkways which are commonly seen as highly distinctive are less Jewish in origin than they may now look. They are customs imported from other regions of the world by Jewish immigration, which in their place of origin would have looked less strange. For example, Hasidic garb on Britain's streets now looks exotically Jewish, but that garb fundamentally is non-Jewish in origin and would have been less characteristically Jewish in the time and place of its origin. And, of course, only a minority of Jews feel the need to go around dressed like a Hasid.

Or take the question of Jewish food. It is easy to go into any large bookshop in the British Isles, and find a series of impressive volumes labelled 'Jewish Cookery'. Inside are all sorts of tasty recipes for dishes which people think of as Jewish, but it is not too hard to distinguish between those elements which simply represent Jewish variations of regional cuisines, and those which are more intimately bound up with Jewish religious tradition, and can only be understood with reference to that tradition. So while I feel I need to find time to say something about *kashrut*, I don't have anything to say in my 'Introduction' about gefilte fish, or chicken soup.

Or take Jewish languages. Jews over the years have adopted a wide variety of languages, and devised their own Jewish versions of them – Jewish Greek (probably), Jewish Aramaic, Judaeo-Arabic, Ladino, as well as numerous regional Jewish patois and jargons. There is a variety of English spoken by Jews among themselves, marked by Yiddishisms and Hebraisms which acts as a strong social marker of Jewish identity in Britain, and which can sometimes be pretty incomprehensible to outsiders. Some of these Jewish languages have been elevated to high religious status by having important religious works composed in them – Aramaic (think of the Targums, the Gemarot, the Zohar, the Kadish), Judaeo-Arabic (think of the Rambam's *Guide of the Perplexed* or his *Commentary on the Mishnah*), Ladino (think of the *Me'am Lo'ez*), Yiddish (think of the *Tze'ena uRe'ena*), but all of these languages pale into insignificance before Hebrew, so in my 'Introduction', while I feel I have to find time to say something about the Holy Tongue, the other languages will get a look-in only if time permits.

If you have followed my train of thought so far, I think it should now be clear that there is a fundamental principle that I am tacitly applying to distinguish between the central and the peripheral in Judaism. In sifting phenomena I am constantly invoking a criterion of universality. The more universal a phenomenon is, the more it qualifies for inclusion in my 'Introduction', because clearly what I should be trying to do is to provide my students with a description of Judaism which is true for the greatest proportion possible of what calls itself Judaism. This universality has three aspects.

(1) First, universality in perception. By this I mean those elements which a majority of Jews – that is to say those who identify themselves as Jews and form in the broadest sense of the term 'the Jewish community' – recognize, on reflection, as central to the definition of Judaism. This recognition does not, it should be noted, necessarily imply acceptance of religious authority or observance, nor even extensive knowledge. Many non-observant Jews, even aggressively secular Jews, would acknowledge that the Tanakh is a central monument of Jewish culture, without for one moment feeling obliged to follow it, in much the same way as educated Englishmen and women might acknowledge the centrality of the King James Bible to English culture.

(2) Second, universality across space. Diaspora has been a fundamental feature of Jewish existence at least since the time of the Babylonian exile, and yet Jews in different parts of the world, in the absence for the most part of institutionalized structures of centralized authority, have achieved an astonishingly high level of mutual recognition. This sense of unity or fellow-feeling has complex causes – one of which is unquestionably external pressure and persecution, but it is also in no small measure due to a genuinely shared Jewish culture. In my 'Introduction' I logically prioritize those shared cultural elements – elements which can be found if my students visit a Jewish community in north Manchester, or Israel, or the States, or North Africa or the Yemen.

(3) Finally, universality over time. I tend to stress those aspects of Judaism today which have deep historical roots, that is to say which can be found stretching back into the Jewish past, which have shown durability and persistence. This helps me to distinguish between the ephemeral or potentially ephemeral and the permanent, though one has, of course, to recognize that innovations in the past have subsequently become permanent features of the tradition. But it is not my job to be a prophet, and I cannot really tell what innovations in the

present may achieve permanency in the future, so I tend to focus on those elements of the present scene which are strongly rooted in the past. When universality in perception, space and time interlock and support each other I feel I have a strong framework within which to present a normative account of Judaism.

Of these persistence over time is for me particularly important. I think this is not just because my training and academic instincts are those of an historian. I would argue that the default position in the academy in the analysis of Judaism or any other religion is the historical. I have found time and again that the best way to give my students an understanding of some aspect of Judaism today is to tell the story of how it came about. I am not in the least decrying other academic approaches – the sociological, the anthropological, the theological, the cultural, and so forth: I try to inform my historical understanding with insights drawn from all these disciplines; but I am constantly struck by how often the practitioners of these other approaches feel the need at some point to digress into history to make sense of their data.

The concept of 'Jewish Tradition'

What in effect I am trying to describe is 'the Jewish tradition', and I confess myself nonplussed by colleagues who dismiss this concept as a meaningless construct. A construct it certainly is, but it is by no means meaningless. It can easily be given substance. I can define it in terms of canonic texts, that is to say texts of high religious authority and cultural significance which feature prominently in Jewish discourse, and are seen as a reference point for belief and practice. Of these, of course, Tanakh is central, but, taking the long view, we should also probably include the Talmud, the Prayerbook, Rashi, the Codes, the Zohar. Just what is classified as canonic is, of course, open to dispute, as are the degrees of canonicity and authority, and also the way the texts should be read. Judaism has developed a sophisticated system of hermeneutics which allows very different forms of Judaism to claim validation from the same canonic texts. What is interesting is the degree to which this canon is genealogical in character, with the later texts 'descending' from the earlier, and making constant reference to them. There are grounds for disagreement, but that certain texts will be universally acknowledged as canonic is surely not open to dispute.

I can also define 'Jewish tradition' institutionally, that is in terms of institutions which over a long period of time have steadily and fundamentally shaped Jewish religious life. One of these is obviously the synagogue. Now we know that the synagogue was not always there. There was a time when the Temple was the focus of Jewish religious life, but certainly since late antiquity the majority of Jews have expressed their communal worship through the synagogue. The synagogue has changed over the centuries – in architecture, in governance, in forms of worship, but once again a genealogical principle applies: I find little difficulty in establishing a historical link between most present-day synagogues and the synagogues of late antiquity. Another key institution of Judaism is the Rabbinate, which like the synagogue has persisted from late antiquity down to the present day, and has seen off fundamental challenges to its authority from Christianity and Qaraism. Its two basic institutions – the Beit Din and the Yeshivah/Rabbinical Seminary in its diverse forms – have played a key role in ensuring the persistence of the Rabbinate and the propagation of its values. Another institution, of a rather different kind, which demonstrates strong persistence is the calendar – the pattern of festivals, fasts and times of prayer which has for so many Jews imposed rhythm and meaning on the flux of time. The present-day calendar again wasn't always there: calendrical diversity was apparently common in Second Temple and early Talmudic times, and there were disputes later as to how the calendar should be calculated, and who had the authority promulgate it, but since the early middle ages the same calendar has prevailed within Judaism and provided an important framework for religious observance.

I also feel able to define 'Jewish tradition' in terms of theological ideas – Torah, God, creation, Israel, redemption. These ideas have been understood in a wide variety of ways, but I think any Jewish theology which failed to address them would be manifestly defective, and despite the varied understandings of the key concepts they still dovetail to form a religious worldview which differentiates Judaism from other religious worldviews – even those of the other so-called Abrahamic faiths.

All the cultural elements I have mentioned are in a sense 'frameworks' or 'vessels' which can contain very diverse content, but there is a limit to their flexibility: they have a strong shape which pre-determines the content that can be put into them – you can break them if you force certain content into them. They interlock to create a nexus of texts, institutions, practices and ideas that form the deep-structure of Judaism as a religion – a structure that has persisted for almost two thousand years – which I regard as my task as a teacher to lay bare in my 'Introduction to Judaism'. I'm not alone in this. I find the majority of academic introductions to Judaism – whatever the standpoint of their authors – take a rather similar view: there is real consensus here.

Norms as an instrument of analysis and evaluation

Identifying the core Jewish tradition is important not just as an exercise in discovering facts (that is, what are the norms). It is not just a description. It provides us with an important analytical and evaluative tool. The norms serve as an instrument by which to measure the centrality or marginality of any given phenomenon that presents itself as Jewish, and as a historian of Judaism I find such measurements important. I realise I am treading now on sensitive and contested ground. There is a widespread view that self-authentication should be the rule in the study of religion in the academy. In other words if any group *says* it is Jewish, or for that matter Christian or Muslim, then, for the academy it *is* Jewish, or Christian or Muslim. It is not for the academy in any way to challenge this claim, or to make value judgements. The academy is not in the business of legitimizing or delegitimizing any form of a religion: its business is to describe, study, understand. There is a great deal of wisdom in this: the academy must resist attempts to manipulate it politically (especially now when all sorts of political, ideological and even religious interests are trying to high-jack its agenda and its authority), and it will be an immense and fruitless distraction if it gets drawn into intra- or inter-communal religious disputes. Nevertheless the academy cannot renounce its right to test and evaluate by the evidence at its disposal the strength of any religious group's claim to belong to and represent authentically any given religious tradition. I shall return to tackle the issues raised here head-on at the end of my paper, but let me explore the problem first by considering a concrete case.

The case of the Beta Israel

I toyed with a number of possibilities that could have made my point – groups which represent differing degrees of marginality within Judaism: the Black Hebrews, Messianic Jews, the Frankists; but I have settled in the end on the Beta Israel, commonly known as the Falashas, the Black Jews of Ethiopia. They are an interesting case, which has deeply divided the Jewish world. The issues are complex and emotive, but I would argue that the academic position is pretty clear. Two preliminary points should be made. The first is that the Beta Israel are an immensely attractive group, and the strength of their self-affirmation as Jewish is profound and unswerving. No-one could fail to be moved by the story of their persecution in Ethiopia, their great Exodus to the Sudan, and their airlift to Israel.[9] The second preliminary point is the extraordinary generosity of Israel and the Jewish community worldwide in finding the resources to rescue them and settle them in Israel. This is a humanitarian effort of which Jewry can be proud. There have been problems of absorption: they have suffered discrimination and sometimes even racism, but the good intentions of the majority of Israelis and of a variety of Israeli governments towards them cannot seriously be questioned. Many of the second generation Ethiopian Jews have integrated successfully, and are making a contribution to Israeli life and culture. But what can an academic historian say on the question of their Jewishness?

The claim that they are Jewish rests fundamentally on a myth of origins which asserts their descent from the tribe of Dan, a myth that was already known to Jews in Europe, North Africa and the Middle East during the middle ages through the curious little treatise of Eldad ha-Dani, who may well have been a genuine Ethiopian Jew. No less a halakhic authority than the Radbaz (1479–1573), on the basis that the myth was true, accepted their Jewishness, and his opinion was to prove important for later halakhic authorities, such as Ezriel Hildesheimer in the nineteenth century (when the Falashas came to the attention of European Jewry through Christian attempts to convert them) and Ovadiah Yosef in the late twentieth century (when their Jewish status in Israeli law was being hotly debated). To put it rather simplistically, the Radbaz based his opinion on the historicity of the Danite origin of the group, and the later halakhic authorities who accepted their Jewishness based *their* opinions on the authority of the Radbaz.[10] But I know of no academic who would entertain for one moment as historically accurate the Danite origin of the Beta Israel. There is simply

---

[9] Gadi Ben-Ezer, *The Ethiopian Exodus: Narratives of the Migration Journey to Israel 1977–1985* (London: Routledge, 2002).

[10] Michael Corinaldi, *Jewish Identity: The Case of Ethiopian Jews* (Jerusalem: Magnes Press, 1998) offers an overview of the legal arguments, and a useful collection of sources. There are two relevant responsa of the Radbaz, and in both he accepts the Danite origin as fact: 'It is well known that there are constant wars among the kings of Cush. There are three kingdoms: part [of the country] is Ishmaelite [Muslim], part is Aramean [Christian] who adhere to their religion, and part is Israelite from the tribe of Dan.' The Jews 'who come from the land of Cush are without doubt of the tribe of Dan'. Ovadiah Yosef also issued two weighty responsa on the subject, in both of which he came down decisively in favour of the Jewishness of the Beta Israel, but his arguments effectively turn on his claim that the halakhic stature of the Radbaz has no equal in this generation and so cannot be overturned by any contemporary halakhic authority (a classic invocation of the doctrine of 'the decline of the generations'). Ashkenazi authorities, such as Rabbi Moshe Feinstein, who question the Jewishness of the Beta Israel, emphasize the historical uncertainty of their Danite origin as an important ground for their opinion.

no evidence of a migration of ancient Danites to the Horn of Africa, and it is, for all sorts of reasons, intrinsically highly unlikely.[11]

The actual historical origins of the Beta Israel are shrouded in mystery. Some have postulated a Jewish migration southwards from Egypt along the Nile: we know of a Jewish colony at Elephantine as early as the Persian period. Others postulate a migration from South Arabia, where we know of significant Jewish communities in the first few centuries CE (for example, in Himyar). Still others have postulated a connection with the old pre-Christian Aksumite Kingdom of northern Ethiopia, which seems to have had strong Hebraic elements in its culture, and possibly a significant ethnic Jewish minority. Most probably, however, the Beta Israel originated much later in a Judaizing movement which broke away from the Ethiopian Church (it is interesting that they share with Ethiopian Christianity the same Ge'ez version of the Bible). In other words the claim that they are descended from ancient Israelites is totally uncorroborated and very implausible.

That in itself may not be too much of problem. Basing Jewish identity on descent has its limitations since, although most people can trace their ancestry back a few generations, few can verify it five or ten generations ago: status based on descent lands one in a *probatio diabolica* – a claim which by its very nature is almost certainly beyond proof. What is much more significant for our present purposes, however, is the fact that the relationship of the Beta Israel to normative Judaism, in the sense that I have sketched it earlier, is weak or non-existent. They have not preserved the Tanakh in Hebrew; their customs and prayers and calendar are significantly different from the rest of Jewry; above all they seem totally unacquainted with Rabbinic tradition: religious authority rests with their priesthood (the *Qessoch*).[12] They know nothing of Talmud and the Codes. They are clearly, then, a very marginal group, and – here is the crucial point – I would find it impossible to begin to assess their significance for the history of Judaism without starting from the premise of their marginality.

The Beta Israel have posed a fundamental challenge to accepted perceptions of Jewish identity in Israel, and for me one of the significant outcomes of this challenge has been to reveal the continuing importance of Rabbinic Judaism for the definition of Jewish identity. Ben Gurion and other founding fathers of the State would probably have liked the Law of Return to have operated effectively in terms of the *olim* self-authenticating their Jewishness, but, as those same politicians realized, Israel, if it was to be successful as a *Jewish* State, had to develop a distinctively Jewish culture. Many proposals were advanced as to how this should be

---

[11] Traditional Beta Israel sources seem, curiously, to know nothing of the claim to Danite origin. That is essentially a western myth (though found in Eldad ha-Dani), which has figured largely in the halakhic debate. Older Beta Israel traditions link their origin to a migration of Jews from Israel in the time of Solomon, who accompanied Menelik, the son of Solomon and Sheba, when he returned to Ethiopia from Jerusalem. This is the story that, apparently, the Beta Israel told James Bruce, the Abyssinian traveller, in the eighteenth century. See also the answer given in the mid-nineteenth century by Abba Yitzhak, the High Priest of Hohuara to Filosseno Luzzato: 'We came in the reign of Solomon. We arrived by way of Sennar, whence we crossed to Aksum ... Clearly we came in the time of Solomon' (Wolf Leslau, *Falasha Anthology: translated from Ethiopic Sources* [New Haven, Conn: Yale University Press, 1987]). This, of course, links the origin of the Jewish community in Ethiopia with the myth of the Solomonic origin of the Royal House of Ethiopia, which is the cornerstone of the *Kebra Negast*. The historicity of this tradition is every bit as problematic as the Danite myth.

[12] Interestingly this fact troubled the Radbaz: 'Evidently they [the Ethiopia Jews] stem from the sect of Zadok and Boethus who are called Qaraites, since they neither know the Oral Torah, nor do they light candles on Sabbath eve' (see Corinaldi quoted above).

done, many experiments inaugurated, but with Israel now more than sixty years old a pattern has surely emerged: Rabbinism plays and will continue to play an important role in that identity. This is obviously true of observant Jews of whatever persuasion, but I would suggest it is also true of many secular and non-observant Israelis as well. I am constantly intrigued how Jewish friends in Israel who would seldom darken the door of a synagogue, nor accept the religious authority of the Rabbinate in their day-to-day lives, nonetheless honour the great texts and figures of the Rabbinic movement as an inalienable part of their cultural heritage. Given all this it is hard to find a place on the Israeli cultural map for a group like the Beta Israel who have absolutely no connection to that Rabbinic past.

This analysis prompts a further observation: we should be in no doubt that accepting, as liberal Israelis demand, the Beta Israel as fully Jewish within the parameters of their own distinctive form of Ethiopian Judaism, has enormous implications for Jewish identity: it expands it significantly; it opens the door to other groups to claim membership of Israel on the basis of their self-authentication as Jewish. If the Beta Israel, why not the Black Hebrews? A thorough-going pluralism towards Jewish identity raises the question as to what would bind the diverse Jewish groups together, other than loyalty to the State of Israel, and defence of its continued existence and way of life. Other countries, with large immigrant populations, have, in effect, settled for this minimal view of national identity, but it raises questions of national cohesion with which politicians of all persuasions have had to wrestle. Now it would take us too far afield to enter into this debate here: suffice to say that I can see no way of meaningfully analysing it without establishing some sort of normative definition of Judaism. It should be said that the Ethiopian Jews, by all accounts, are meanwhile resolving the conundrum themselves. While Ethiopian folkways persist among them, significant numbers are abandoning their traditional Beta Israel practices and becoming secular, and in some cases even tragically alienated from Israeli society. Others are adapting their Beta Israel traditions to Rabbinic Judaism, a move accelerated by the fact that some *Qessoch* are beginning to attend Yeshivah. This rabbinization of Ethiopian Judaism is by no means new: it goes all the way back to the work of Jacques Faitlovitch even before the Ethiopian *ʿaliyyah* to Israel.[13]

Implications beyond the academy?

I will conclude by returning briefly to the thorny problem of whether normativity as determined by academic criteria and academic analysis, and normativity as claimed within the faith communities carry any implications for each other? This is an aspect of a much wider question of the relationship between the academy on the one hand, and the religious traditions and communities it studies on the other, and it applies as much to Christianity and Islam as to Judaism. It is in these wider terms that I would like to canvass the issues. For sound practical reasons a standoff has developed between the academy and the faith communities over the past hundred years in which each side jealously guards the autonomy of its own domain. The academy is prickly about any attempt by the faith communities to influence its

---

[13] See Emanuela Trevisan Semi, *Father of the Falashas: The Life of Jacques Faitlovich* (London: Vallentine Mitchell, 2007).

deliberations. The faith communities are equally prickly if the academy dares to trespass on their patch. Each has its own truth and exercises its own authority in its own sphere. And maybe it is best to leave it at that. The last thing we want to do is to re-ignite the wars of science and religion, of reason and revelation, which raged in the nineteenth century. But a philosophical problem remains. Do we jettison, then, any notion of the unity of truth? Is truth purely contextual? There is one truth for religion and another for the academy? Neither side traditionally has been prepared to accept that: each has regarded its claims as universally valid. To put it more concretely, what happens in those cases where the religious traditions make historical claims (and the Abrahamic religions as historical religions make many historical claims) which the academy, for well-founded reasons, would question? Can the academic objections simply be dismissed or ignored? This is essentially the age-old problem of the relationship between faith and reason – a problem which has been debated *within* normative Judaism at least from the time of Sa'adya. It is still a problem today, a problem grown more acute in recent years with the rise of fundamentalism of various kinds within the faith communities, which exacerbate the tense relationship between the academy and the religion. I am not about to suggest how the academic study of religion should affect the faith communities. I don't know. But of one thing I am persuaded: the academy and the faith communities are, whether they like it or not, locked into a relationship, and the sooner they begin to recognize, assess and negotiate that relationship the better it will be for all concerned.

BIBLIOGRAPHY

Austin, J.L., *The Province of Jurisprudence Determined* (London: Weidenfeld and Nicolson, 1971).

Baeck, Leo, *The Essence of Judaism* (New York: Schocken Books, 1961).

Ben-Ezer, Gadi, *The Ethiopian Exodus: Narratives of the Migration Journey to Israel 1977–1985* (London: Routledge, 2002).

Biale, David, *Gershom Scholem: Kabbalah and Counter History* 2nd ed. (Cambridge, Mass: Harvard University Press, 1982).

Corinaldi, Michael, *Jewish Identity: The Case of Ethiopian Jews* (Jerusalem: Magnes Press, 1998).

Dan, Joseph, *Gershom Scholem and the Mystical Dimension of Judaism* (New York: New York University Press, 1988).

Hayek, F., *Law, Legislation and Liberty* (London: Routledge & Kegan Paul, 1969).

Leslau, Wolf, *Falasha Anthology: translated from Ethiopic Sources* (New Haven, Conn: Yale University Press, 1987).

Mendes-Flohr, P.R., and Jehuda Reinharz, eds., *The Jew in the Modern World: A Documentary History* (New York: Oxford University Press, 1980).

Neusner, Jacob, *Studying Classical Judaism: A Primer* (Louisville, Kentucky: Westminster/John Knox Press, 1991).

Rotenstreich, Nathan, 'Symbolism and Transcendence: On Some Philosophical Aspects of Gershom Scholem's Opus', *The Review of Metaphysics* 31 (1978).

Scholem, G., *Sabbatai Sevi: The Mystical Messiah* (Princeton: Princeton University Press, 1976).

Schweid, Eliezer, *Judaism and Mysticism according to Gershom Scholem: A Critical Analysis and Programmatic Discussion*, trans. David Avraham Weiner (Atlanta, Georgia: Scholars Press, 1985).

Trevisan Semi, Emanuela, *Father of the Falashas: The Life of Jacques Faitlovich* (London: Vallentine Mitchell, 2007).

MAIMONIDEAN MARGINS

Daniel Davies*

Moses Maimonides is a central figure who would figure prominently in many accounts of normative Judaism. There are also ways in which he is marginal. He operated between different traditions of thought, placing him on the margins of each. His *Guide for the Perplexed* is a work that draws upon them all. It is sometimes thought to represent a non-normative Judaism which it hides behind a veneer of traditional belief. However, the reasons offered for this view should be put down to the fact that it was written in order to update the rabbinic tradition into a new idiom appropriate for a new time; Maimonides operated on the margins between different eras. Furthermore, despite his importance for Judaism his ideas have often been marginal to Judaism because they draw on universal philosophical ideas and thus allegedly encourage apostasy. Those who criticise him for practising philosophy fail to distinguish between universal philosophical norms and the ability of particular people to access those norms.

Maimonides' *Guide for the Perplexed* lends itself to use as a springboard by later thinkers to advance their own theology. In this paper I will suggest that what makes the *Guide* receptive to such updated readings is its position near certain boundaries, and that engaging with it in a constructive manner today calls less for a normative belief than a certain attitude towards those boundaries, an attitude that is a reaction to stagnant norms and a challenge to a static Judaism. To take Maimonides as marginal, may seem strange. This is the same person who, it is often said, wrote the first list of dogmas for rabbinic Judaism, and one which seems to have gained acceptance amongst a large part of the Jewish community.[1] His law code is so important that there are notes referring to its relevant sections in the margins of the classic Bomberg editions of the Talmud, but that is not the only place where Maimonides can be found in the margins. There are those who wish to sideline philosophy and, with it, much of Maimonides' work. So the first of the ways in which Maimonides' *Guide* might be considered marginal arises from those who object to it as philosophy, raising the question of whether or not it could even be considered part of a normative Judaism at all.

Maimonides had many critics and amongst them was the fifteenth century Shem-Toḇ ibn Shem-Toḇ. He faced up to them during his own lifetime and, shortly after his death, the so called 'Maimonidean controversy' erupted, focussing on his alleged heresy.[2] Even within this context Shem Toḇ's attack stands out in articulating many of the reasons why people felt uncomfortable with what they thought philosophy teaches. For example, he explains what he

---

* Research Associate, Talyor-Schechter Genizah Research Unit. Email: did20@cam.ac.uk

[1] Marc Shapiro points out that they are not the first principles, though they are the best known. *The Limits of Orthodox Theology: Maimonides' Thirteen Principles Reappraised* (Oxford, Portland Oregon: The Littman Library of Jewish Civilization, 2004), 4.

[2] See Idit Dobbs-Weinstein, 'The Maimonidean Controversy', *History of Jewish Philosophy* (London: Routledge, 1997), 331–349.

takes to be the philosophers' position regarding the world to come.[3] He reports that they make eternal life dependent upon intellectual knowledge, rather than on fulfilling commands. Consequently, argues Shem-Tob, the wicked person who perfects his intellect is assured a place in their afterlife, while the saintly but ignorant God-fearing Jew is excluded. But the philosophers go further. They interpret the prophecies and the deepest secrets of the Torah as if scripture teaches nothing more than Greek science. What is worse is that they argue that a philosopher is superior to a prophet, since the philosopher says clearly what the prophet says in riddles. Furthermore, they say that the prophets made mistakes since science had not been perfected in their times.[4] Shem-Tob writes as follows: 'when I investigated their words, as far as I was able, a mighty flame burned within me because a malignant leprosy has flowered amongst the children of Israel.' He goes on to blame the decline in his own community on the philosophers. They 'twisted the tabernacle, and burst through its fences. The people followed them until our bones had dried out and our hope was lost, since they concluded that there is no judgement nor accounting over good and evil.'[5]

But the *Guide* evinces disparate attitudes in its readers, so that others consider its author to be the epitome of mainstream Jewish thought. For example, Shem-Tob's grandson was a staunch Maimonidean who is now best known for an extensive commentary on the *Guide for the Perplexed*. Shem-Tob ben Joseph ben Shem-Tob ibn Shem-Tob appended two highly allusive poems to his introduction, the first of which reads as follows:[6]

למורה כמורה עלי עץ ודשא וממי מרי מש מתי שוא ותשי
והוא ראש ובן ראש עדי ראש ואחי והוא רב ובן רב עדי רב רב ואשי
והגביר בריתו וכפר בדתו עונות עדתו בקרכן ואשה
למענו חרונו אלוהי מעונו יעורר ודינו יהי עז וקשה
ויאמר לצריו ושורפי ספריו אני קם ולא א חריש עוד ואחשה
בשומכם לשונכם בנביא וכי לא יראתם לדבר בעבדי במשה

The *Guide* refreshing as first autumn rains, beyond lakes of suspicion of the worthless and weak
A leader and head adorns heads and my kin, a rabbi whose line sees Rav and Ashi bejeweled
He strengthened God's pact through his religion atoned like sacrificial fire his congregation's
    misdeeds
For his sake the God of his support will kindle his wrath judging mighty and harsh
He will say to his foes who are burning his books *I arise and will no longer keep quiet*
When you sharpen your tongues to slander the prophet and fear not to speak of my servant Moshe.

This poem seems to be an appropriate introduction since it recalls in several ways the *Guide*'s own introduction. First, when he writes that it is an embellishment adorning Rav and Ashi, the heads of the Geonic academies at Sura and Pumbedita, Shem Tob connects the the *Guide* and the Talmud. The last line of the poem is even clearer: any who speak against Maimonides speak against 'Moses our master', so on this reading the *Guide* is very much a

---

[3] Shem Tob ibn Shem Tob, *Sefer Emunot* (Ferrara: Abraham ibn Ushki, 1556), 4r. Herbert Davidson briefly discusses Shem Tob's attack in *Moses Maimonides: The Man and his Works* (New York: Oxford University Press, 2005), 414–415.

[4] On this point see Charles Touati's 'Le problème de l'inerrance prophétique dans la théologie juive du Moyen Age', *Revue de L'Histoire des Religions* 174 (1968), 169–187.

[5] *Sefer Emunot*, 4r.

[6] Shem Tob's commentary often appears alongside Ibn Tibbon's translation. I have used R. Mosis Maimonidis *More Nebuchim (Doctor Perplexorum) ex versione Samuelis Tibbonidae cum commentariis Ephodaei, Schemtob, Ibn Crescas, nec non Don Isaci Abravanel asjectis summariis et indicibus* (Berlin: Adolf Cohn Verlag und Antiquariat, 1875). The poem is on 2v.

part of the Mosaic tradition. Secondly, Shem To<u>b</u> mentions the decline of his own community, which Maimonides is opposing in God's name. For Shem-To<u>b</u>, then, there is nothing marginal about the *Guide*. Nevertheless, these aspects of Maimonides' introduction reveal other ways in which he could be said to inhabit margins, especially those between changing eras and between various traditions.

Even a cursory look at the introduction to the *Guide* reveals that Maimonides is conscious of standing within a tradition and also of the need to update it. He argues that the rabbis presented their views in particular ways that were appropriate for their audience, or, rather, their multiple audiences.[7] However, Maimonides thought that the situation had changed since the time that the midrash and talmud were compiled and another manner of expression was required in order to render the texts into an idiom appropriate for his time. To justify such action he uses two proof-texts: 'it is time to act for the Lord';[8] 'let all your actions be for the sake of heaven'.[9] Maimonides' use of these sentiments calls to mind Jonathan ben Uzziel's defence against a divine accusation. When Jonathan translated the prophets into Aramaic 'the land of Israel shook over 400 square parasangs and a heavenly voice said 'Who is this who has revealed my secrets to humankind?' Jonathan replies as follows: 'It is I who revealed your secrets to humankind, but it is revealed and known to you that I did not do so for my own honour, nor for my family's honour, but I did it for your honour, so that arguments among Israelites would not multiply.'[10] Whether or not Maimonides has this passage in mind, the implication is that he considers himself to be on the threshold of a new era requiring a new kind of access to the tradition. Like Jonathan, he translates for the requirement of a new time and his motives are pure.

For the *Guide* to work as a commentary it needs to be treated as part of the tradition of sacred texts on which it is commenting, and so it needs to be treated with respect and sympathy. Maimonides explicitly asks the reader to approach his *Guide* in such a way as to consider it a genuine and honest attempt to understand rather than merely an attempt to impose alien ideas. So he asks those who receive no benefit from the book to pretend it was never written. He asks his reader not to be overly hasty in objecting to his words 'for that which he understood might be contrary to my intention'.[11] Whoever believes that there is a mistake in the *Guide* should adopt a charitable view and, quoting the Mishnah, Maimonides adjures him to judge favourably.[12] He then states his belief that all who read the *Guide* will find in it something of use. Given the earlier request to ignore it altogether if there is nothing useful, perhaps Maimonides wishes to refer here to people who adopt his advice. This advice describes an attitude necessary for using the *Guide* for the purpose Maimonides wrote it. He is trying to tell us that it needs to be approached in the same way as one approaches the Torah and other traditional texts. They are all supposed to be grappled with and understood in a charitable way. If one fails to see the point of a certain text or parable, it shouldn't

---

[7] *Guide* 5 (15–18), 9.

[8] *Guide* 10 (29), 16. References to the Guide are to page and line numbers of Munk's Judaeo-Arabic edition (Jerusalem: Azriel, 1929) followed by the page number in Pines' translation (Chicago: Chicago University Press, 1963). For an account of the way in which this saying is used in rabbinic literature to explain suspending particular laws see Eliezer Berkovits's *Not in Heaven: The Nature and Function of Halakha* (New York: KTAV, 1983), 64–70.

[9] *Guide* 11 (1), 16.

[10] BT Megillah, 3a.

[11] *Guide* 10 (9), 15.

[12] *Guide* 10 (13), 15.

simply be dismissed. Rather, one should offer it the benefit of the doubt and continue thinking about what the deeper message might be. This is a model of how sacred works are read, and also what Maimonides asks of his own readers.

Another thing Maimonides asks of his prospective students is that they 'learn everything that ought to be learned and constantly study this Treatise. For it will then elucidate for you most of the obscurities of the law.'[13] The only way to benefit fully from the *Guide* is to read other works alongside it, including rabbinic texts as well as the scientific writings of the Arabs. He alludes to all kinds of works, including many dealing with scientific issues. Indeed, on several occasions he reminds the readers not to expect the *Guide* to act as a scientific work, since his purpose is not to write such a work.[14] Rather, his purpose is to write a commentary on scripture and the rabbis. Maimonides hints that certain passages of the *Guide*, and consequently of scripture, can be understood through ideas in other books to which he alludes by providing 'pointers' and 'reminders' to writers as diverse as Avicenna, who was associated with an Aristotelian movement, and the Brethren of Purity, who were authors of anonymous treatises professing very different doctrines.[15] So the sages' advice to 'turn it and turn it, for everything is in it'[16] can apply to the *Guide* as well. Only by reading it alongside all of those other works, and constantly thinking about them in relation to one another, can one hope to reap its full rewards: only thus can it be used as a true *Guide* 'refreshing' tradition as the rains refresh the withered grass, to return to Shem Tob's poem.

Furthermore, the advice is necessary because Maimonides aims to provide a text that imitates the tradition, updating it into an idiom appropriate for his own time. As part of this update the *Guide* attempts to imitate oral teaching, which is the kind of instruction the rabbinic texts advocate when one is teaching difficult matters.[17] There are certain advantages to teaching someone in person. When faced by a pupil, a teacher can assess the pupil's level and decide accordingly what to say and how to say it. The teacher can also respond to individual needs. So an aim of the *Guide* must be to enable it to work in the same fashion as oral instruction when all the above advice for how to approach it correctly is heeded. But the update involves more than imitating oral teaching. Maimonides also needs to imitate the way in which the rabbis' ideas are written up. So the *Guide* is a multi-layered commentary on a multi-layered text. It is written with multiple levels of meaning and using a variety of registers of discourse that reflect both the Bible and the rabbinic literature. Maimonides attempts to duplicate the different levels in his own work because he thinks that scripture is written with all those meanings in mind. From the point of view of the aims of the *Guide*, then, what is important is less the inner meaning of the *Guide* itself than the inner meaning of scripture, even though Maimonides presumably would consider them to be the same.

---

[13] *Guide* 10 (3–4), 15.

[14] *Guide* 176 (3), 253.

[15] Avicenna's work is present in much of the *Guide*. Alexander Altmann explains a particularly famous example in 'Essence and Existence in Maimonides' in Buijs, ed., *Maimonides: A Collection of Critical Essays* (Notre Dame: University of Notre Dame Press, 1988), 148–165. A probable allusion to the Pure Brethren is mentioned by Langermann in 'Maimonides' Repudiation of Astrology', *Maimonidean Studies* 2 (1991), 148.

[16] Abot 5:27

[17] See the first chapter of José Faur's *Homo Mysticus: A Guide to Maimonides' Guide for the Perplexed* (New York: Syracuse University Press, 1998) for examples of similar attitudes in the rabbinic tradition, which Maimonides attempts to imitate.

Requiring the reader to think independently and read widely, connecting outside study to learning the *Guide*, ensures that the student will be able to progress as far as is merited. That is one way in which the tradition is updated for the needs of the hour. For the most part, the outside texts that Maimonides would expect the student to read are philosophical and scientific. There is nothing innovative in Maimonides' reading philosophy into sacred texts nor in his expecting the student to work at deciphering a text. It may be the case, though, that Maimonides' *Guide* is the supreme example of both of these together in the Jewish tradition. Nevertheless, despite Maimonides' own disavowal of scientific originality, he needs to find a new way of expressing certain interpretations of the tradition. Famously, Maimonides lists seven different causes of contradictions in his introduction, and explains that any contradictions occurring in the *Guide* result from the fifth or the seventh.[18] The fifth is used by other philosophers and has a didactic function, Maimonides explains, but the seventh is used only in the *Guide*. This seventh contradiction sets Maimonides' *Guide* apart from preceding works, and is one cause of the variety of interpretations, though not the only one. Maimonides says that it results from an author's need to conceal something from the masses, for which purpose a device is used. So there is something that Maimonides wants to hide from most people. A common view that there is a conflict between religion and philosophy is therefore taken to be indicated by the seventh contradiction.[19]

The idea that philosophy is outside of religious norms made its way into studies of Maimonides. It is often thought that he could not really have been both a philosopher and an advocate of Judaism. His influence is felt in this regard in twentieth century scholarship of Islamic philosophy as well, though through a circuitous route. Dimitri Gutas identifies three major strands of interpretations of Arabic philosophy that are distorted through an Orientalist lens. All three have their analogues in Maimonidean studies, and one in particular seems to take its cue from Maimonides, or, rather, a particular interpretation of Maimonides. It is often labelled 'Straussian' because it builds upon Leo Strauss' insistence that there is an irreconcilable conflict between religion and philosophy.[20] A major concern of philosophers, then, is to hide their philosophical tendencies behind a veneer of traditional religious belief. Sometimes the impression given by this approach is that 'medieval Arabic philosophy was in fact nothing else but a continuous squabble through and across the centuries about the relative truth values of religion and philosophy.'[21] Gutas argues that the Straussian school of Maimonidean interpretation is an expression of an Orientalist mindset that read its own conflict between religion and reason back into the mediaeval Islamic thinkers.[22]

The Straussian view is based on an assumption that there was a fear of philosophy, which Gutas seems to suggest never existed. Strauss argues that philosophers hide their opinions for fear of the persecution that would follow. His assumption that philosophy and religion

---

[18] The fifth is caused by a teacher's need to explain something in different ways at different stages of a pupil's education. *Guide* II (20), 17. The seventh is the result of the need to conceal something from the masses. *Guide* I2 (7), 18.

[19] Leo Strauss is the most famous example of this school of thought. See his *Persecution and the Arts of Writing* (Chicago: University of Chicago Press, 1988).

[20] For the purposes of this paper, there is no need to enter into a discussion of the relative merits or problems with Strauss, Straussianisms, or the question of how far they accord with one another. For a sympathetic and sensible appraisal see Steven Smith's *Reading Leo Strauss* (Chicago and London: The University of Chicago Press, 2006).

[21] 'The Study of Arabic Philosophy in the Twentieth Century: An Essay on the Historiography of Arabic Philosophy', *British Journal of Middle Eastern Studies* 29 (2002), 9.

[22] Gutas, 10.

oppose each other is based on that of Shem-To<u>b</u> ibn Shem-To<u>b</u> so, whilst it is not necessarily Maimonides' or the Arabs', it predates the enlightenment and the Orientalists.[23] Even if philosophers in the Islamicate were not persecuted because they practised philosophy, there is no doubt that there were Jews in Christian Europe who were suspicious of philosophy. Scholars of Maimonides, even some who claim to be followers of Maimonides, then, have taken on board the anti-Maimonidean tendency to oppose philosophy to religion. This view in turn influenced attitudes to Islamic thought. In that case the Straussian school is influenced less by Maimonides than by the anti-Maimonideans. Philosophy is marginalised through the actions of its opponents, and then its advocates too seem to have taken on board the view that philosophy is opposed to Judaism.

The seventh cause of contradictions is the reason why Gutas locates Strauss' inspiration in the *Guide*, at least in part correctly, and the reason why Gutas may be too hasty in dismissing any methodical innovation at all on the part of Maimonides. I agree that Maimonides does not use the seventh cause of contradictions to hide a philosophical position that opposes the religion of the common people. Philosophy might not be for everyone, but it does not therefore follow that philosophy and religion really do conflict. Rather, as I argue extensively elsewhere, the seventh contradiction is a function of Maimonides' commentary on scripture.[24] There are conflicts and contradictions between the inner meanings of different parts of scripture since, as mentioned above, there are multiple voices in scripture. If Shem To<u>b</u> ibn Shem To<u>b</u>'s claim that the philosophers think that the prophets made mistakes is true, a claim mentioned above, one of the things being hidden might be that there are times when Maimonides is less charitable towards the prophets than he asks his readers to be towards himself. The seventh contradiction is a signal of the need to serve different eras with the same rabbinic tradition, rather than a signal of a rupture between philosophy and religion. It needs to be seen as part of this update.

One Muslim thinker whose image may have suffered from a tendency to draw stark divisions between philosophy and religion is al-Ghazālī. The work he is most famous for in the West is *The Incoherence of the Philosophers*, though he exerted far more influence on the Muslim tradition through others. At the beginning of the *Incoherence* Ghazālī writes as follows:

> I have seen a group who, believing themselves in possession of a distinctiveness from companion
> and peer by virtue of a superior quick wit and intelligence, have rejected the Islamic duties . . .

---

[23] Kraemer says that there is evidence that Maimonides feared persecution. 'How (not) to read the *Guide* of the Perplexed', *Jerusalem Studies in Arabic and Islam* 32 (2006), 358. The evidence he adduces is from a letter Maimonides wrote in which he asked his student to be careful whom he shares certain sections of the *Guide* with, 'so that I am not harmed by the non-Jews or by the many wicked Israelites.' Baneth, ed., *Letters of Maimonides* (Jerusalem: Mekize Nirdamim, 1946). Why Maimonides feared that he would come to harm is unclear from this statement, though. Kraemer argues that Suhrawardi's execution, probably in 1191, explains 'Maimonides's discretion in the *Guide*.' 'Moses Maimonides: An Intellectual Portrait', *The Cambridge Companion to Maimonides* (Cambridge: Cambridge University Library, 2005), 31. However, it is generally thought that Suhrawardi was killed for political reasons. If his ideas troubled the authorities, they would probably have done so because of their resemblance to Ismaʿīlī notions held by the recently deposed Fāṭimid dynasty, rather than because they used philosophy. See John Walbridge, *The Leaven of the Ancients: Suhrawardī and the Heritage of the Greeks* (Albany: State University of New York Press, 2000), 201–210. Finally, the fact that Maimonides exhorts the recipient to be cautious indicates that if there is something for which he might be persecuted in the *Guide* that would be clear to whomever it reaches. Such persecution would not occur because of a secret, hidden doctrine that can be detected only by the initiates but, rather, because of something that can be understood from the text itself.

[24] See my *Method and Metaphysics in Maimonides' Guide*, in the AAR series *Reflection and Theory in the Study of Religion* published by Oxford University Press.

they have entirely cast off the reins of religion through multifarious beliefs . . . [this is] an outcome of their stumbling over the tails of sophistical doubts that divert from the direction of truth . . . The source of their unbelief is their hearing high-sounding names such as Socrates, Hippocrates, Plato, Aristotle, and their likes, and the exaggeration and misguidedness of groups of their followers in describing their minds, the excellence of their principles, the exactitude of their geometrical, logical, natural, and metaphysical sciences and in [describing these as] being alone – by reason of excessive intelligence and acumen – [capable] of extracting these hidden things.[25]

Here Ghazālī expresses an apparent opposition to philosophy, namely that it is opposed to religion because it encourages believers to diminish the importance they place on religious practice and even to abandon religious faith altogether. Nevertheless, it is becoming increasingly recognised that Ghazālī was no simple opponent of philosophy in the manner of Shem-Tob ibn Shem-Tob. What he criticised in the *Incoherence* is philosophers' excesses, as he saw them. Philosophy in itself, and correctly deployed, is not to be dismissed; Ghazālī himself makes considerable use of it in other contexts.[26] Like Maimonides, Ghazālī is an enigmatic figure who influenced later religious traditions enormously. Ebrahim Moosa argues that the reason he was able to exert such influence on later generations is his use of such a great variety of different and different kinds of thought which he wove together into an integrated whole.[27] He stood in the liminal space between different traditions and ideas, evaluating each on the basis of the ideas themselves rather than on the basis of their provenance, and incorporating those he accepted into a whole. This is a model of a way in which a great thinker can engage with tradition, attempting to respect that tradition's borders whilst using all resources, both from the tradition and an individual's own intellectual resources, in a creative way appropriate to a challenge facing a living community.

As explained above, in his introduction Maimonides advocates the same kind of approach. Like al-Ghazālī he inhabited a space between different intellectual traditions, rabbinic and philosophical. He too tried to engage honestly with all of them. His attitude could be summed up by the the the poet Dunash ibn-Labrat's motto, 'let scripture be your Eden, and the Arabs' books your paradise grove'.[28] Maimonides weaves sections from diverse sources into the treatise. Often it is difficult to see how they fit together. Sometimes they almost certainly do not. He is not providing a philosophical system: that does not mean that he does not have one; it simply means that his purpose in the *Guide* is not to present it.[29] Instead, he is explaining scripture, and scripture speaks with many voices. Some of those voices are in conflict with each other. So Maimonides advances several different positions, drawing upon a variety of schools of thought and kinds of writings, creating conflicting accounts of how the world works. Some of the conflict, though, is presented in a way that makes it difficult to detect and is made more so by the use of 'devices' to hide the 'inner' meaning of the *Guide* and, therefore, of scripture. This method of drawing upon different traditions and different sources enables Maimonides to connect his *Guide* with the Jewish tradition since, as already

---

[25] Al Ghazālī, *The Incoherence of the Philosophers*. A parallel English-Arabic text translated, introduced and annotated by Michael E. Marmura (Provo, Utah: Brigham Young University Press, 1997), 2.

[26] Richard Frank has mapped some similarities between al-Ghazālī and one of his targets, Avicenna, in *Creation and the Cosmic System: Al-Ghazālī & Avicenna* (Heidelberg: Carl Winter, 1992).

[27] *Ghazālī and the Poetics of Imagination* (Chapel Hill: The University of North Carolina Press, 2005).

[28] As translated in Peter Cole's *The Dream of the Poem: Hebrew Poetry from Muslim and Christian Spain* (Princeton and Oxford: Princeton University Press, 2007), 24.

[29] *Guide* 176 (3–7), 253.

noted, it requires an approach that is religious in attitude; it requires one to continue meditating on the material presented and judge it in a positive light. If one is to conclude that an idea is worthless, one ought to abandon it, at least temporarily, or presume that there is something more to it that is not yet understood, and continue to seek out its value. Aside from a traditional, Jewish attitude, this is also a perfect example of what has been called 'a fundamental philosophical attitude, combining humility with realism.'[30] Philosophy demands humility and patience. Far from religion and philosophy opposing each other, then, thinkers like Maimonides and Ghazālī present them as in concord, but only when the limits of human understanding are properly drawn.

Could the anti-Maimonidean movement that Shem-Ṭob represents be a reaction to 'radical' interpretations of Maimonides rather than to Maimonides himself, just as Ghazālī's difficulty was with what he perceived to be the abuse of philosophy, rather than the very use of it? In that case, if philosophy is to be taken in an appropriate and 'religious' way, there would be no need to object to it.[31] But Shem-Ṭob's opposition goes deeper than this. He disagrees with Maimonides' very claim that reason and philosophy can enhance one's understanding of Judaism. So in Shem-Ṭob's opinion, the problem is not that the philosophers go too far, but the very practice of philosophy. He expresses his surprise at Maimonides for justifying 'most of the commandments by way of the philosophers' characteristics (מדות) and the rest on backward nations (עמים נופלים) so that none are intended in their own right.'[32] Here he objects to explanations of the commandments that make them dependent upon a goal, referring to two in particular. The first explains that certain commandments are means by which characteristics can be trained and virtues instilled in a person. The second explains that others were established in order to lead people away from idolatrous practices that were common at the time. The practices are not good in themselves, only insofar as they serve a good purpose. So, for example, Maimonides argues that the laws about sacrifices were commanded because the people lived in an environment in which sacrifices were widely practised as a form of worship. They were adapted to the service of God.[33] Once again, however, the practise of sacrificing is not good in itself; it is only good inasmuch as it brings about a good outcome. That is why Shem-Ṭob thinks it follows from the philosophers' position that there is no judgement, and that is why he blames Maimonides in particular whose 'books and claims were the reasons for the Israelites' denial of the God of their fathers.'[34]

Neglect of the law's importance is a strange charge to level at philosophers. They are concerned with living ethical lives and with the consequences of their actions. They are concerned with the negative influence any excesses may have upon their characters. The law is a very important way to avoid these negative influences and to encourage growth and improvement in physical habits, moral characteristics and intellectual-spiritual abilities. This

---

[30] Marcel Dubois *Temps et l'instant Selon Aristote* (Paris: Desclée de Brouwer, 1967), 370. I am grateful to David Burrell for pointing me to this source.

[31] This is the import of some of Isaac Abrabanel's writings. For example, he defends Maimonides' view of creation from some who distort it but claim to represent it faithfully, thus reclaiming the master from his purported disciples. See Seymour Feldman's *Philosophy in a time of Crisis: Don Isaac Abravanel, Defender of the Faith* (London and New York: RoutledgeCurzon, 2003), 40–66.

[32] *Sefer Emunot*, 15v.

[33] *Guide* 384 (19), 526.

[34] *Sefer Emunot*, 15v.

is certainly Maimonides' view. It is also Aristotle's view; although he didn't have the Mosaic law, law is the way in which he thought that people ought to regulate themselves in order to facilitate their own perfection.[35] So Shem To<u>b</u>'s disagreement cannot be based on the idea that the philosophers ignore the law's importance but on their practise of offering rationales for the commandments. Maimonides is absolutely opposed to the view that reasons in principle intelligible to all should not be offered for the commandments. He claims that refusing the existence of rational explanations diminishes rather than augments their importance. Unlike Shem-To<u>b</u>, he says that the commandments have a purpose beyond themselves, so they are not ends in their own right. Simple observance is too easy and insufficient.[36] To worship God properly requires intellectual effort that goes far beyond practice alone.[37]

Jose Faur objects to the claim that philosophy and Judaism are opposed to one another. He also objects to Shem-To<u>b</u> ibn Shem-To<u>b</u>'s assertion that a rise in philosophy was to blame for the decline of the Jewish community and for mass apostasy. Rather, in Faur's view, the anti-Maimonideans are to blame for the decline of the Jewish community.[38] He points out that many of the apostates were not philosophers, but products of the school that opposed philosophy. Furthermore, in those places where Maimonides became the main authority, such as in Yemen, there was no such mass defection.[39] Faur explains that the kind of Judaism that the anti-Maimonideans opposed is one which is in full accord with philosophy. It is one in which, in the halakhic realm, decisions can be based upon arguments and evidence. Consequently the reasons for any particular ruling are transparent to all who train their intellects correctly. The ruling is open to challenges and objections from any who might think that it is based upon unsound reasoning or false principles. Training in intellectual discipline is necessary in order to assess them, but it is clear what the rules of debate are. By contrast, a characteristic of those who oppose philosophy is to base their rulings on obscure origins, often on the inscrutable whim of a powerful individual. Faur documents the methods used by the anti-Maimonideans to sideline such discussion by preventing the opposing view from receiving a fair hearing.[40] Often they took the form of threats. These methods are repugnant to Judaism, in Faur's view. The Palestinian Talmud also tells of an occasion when such a technique was used, resulting in a fatal dispute. Rabbi Joshua Onayya reported that students of Bet Shammai killed students of Bet Hillel. While six students of Bet Shammai went to discuss rulings in an upper chamber, the rest remained below with swords and spears, presumably to prevent students of Bet Hillel from having their say. That day was said to be as bad for Israel as the day the golden calf was built.[41] God is said to have wanted to destroy the Israelites when they made the calf, so the passage presents an extremely strong condemnation of violence as a means of asserting authority (Exod. 32 and Deut. 9). Faur offers an attractive account of authentic Jewish ways of reading texts, based upon logical and philosophical rigour. It may be an idealised version. The kind

---

[35] *Nichomacean Ethics* X, 9.

[36] This is clear from *Guide* 84 (3), 123.

[37] Kenneth Seeskin explains why a focus on obedience to the exclusion of understanding is too easy in *Maimonides: A Guide for Today's Perplexed* (West Orange: Behrman House, 1991), 122–124.

[38] Jose Faur, 'Anti-Maimonidean Demons', *Review of Rabbinic Judaism* 6 (2003).

[39] Ibid., 4.

[40] Ibid., 5–14.

[41] PT Shabbat 1.4.

of interpretation that he explains seems close to the method of *ʻiyyun* that arose after the expulsion and drew on Islamic philosophy.[42] In any case, what is important is that the kind of discussion such a method of study opens up is intelligible and logical; whether or not it is historically accurate, the point still stands. Philosophy is in principle a discipline open to anyone who has the opportunity and the patience to study it.[43] The reason anti-Maimonideans are responsible for the decline of Iberian Jewry is, in Faur's view, that they shifted the basis of authority from knowledge and argumentation to individual intuition.[44] The basis of authority thereby became both arbitrary and incontestable.

Another way to express the difference in attitude towards authority is suggested by the work of another scholar of Maimonides, Menachem Kellner. He locates a key in the doctrine of the pre-existence of the Torah, which has several ramifications.[45] For example, Maimonides assessed the scientific views of the prophets and the rabbis in exactly the same way as he assessed any other scientific views. If scientific evidence indicates that the sages were mistaken about something he sides with the scientific evidence, not with the sages or even the prophets.[46] As mentioned above, that is exactly one of the things to which Shem-Tob ibn Shem-Tob objected. The Mishnah states that the Torah is a העולם נברא שבו כלי, a 'blueprint for creation'.[47] Kellner points out that if the world is created through a pre-existent Torah, it can be inferred that the world should be understood by way of the Torah. Therefore, anything perceived as coming from outside it is unimportant and should be, at best, subordinated to the Torah.[48] However, those who reject the idea, Maimonides among them, are not entitled to draw such a conclusion. Rather, for them the reverse is true: the way to understand the world is to investigate the world itself. The Torah can only be understood against the background of the world in which it was revealed, a world which pre-existed the Torah. As mentioned above, the kind of understanding and reading of texts the *Guide* requires, because of the way it is written and the ideals it encourages, accords with the idea that the Torah must be understood by a thoughtful person who reads whatever is worthwhile, no matter where such writings are found or who wrote them. This is also the kind of reading and understanding that Faur considers more authentic to the Jewish tradition, a tradition which is open to understanding and encourages spiritual and intellectual development, just like the *Guide* and the philosophers.[49] Faur in effect argues that the attempt to inhabit such a marginal space is a normative, authentic, Jewish attitude, although inhabiting the margins has been pushed out to the margins.

Both Kellner and Faur are in favour of the respective aspects of Maimonides' attitude towards authority upon which they elaborate. They both argue that Maimonides' opponents have had a damaging effect upon Jewish life. Furthermore, I think that Kellner's ideas can provide a way of explaining the kind of attitude towards authority that Faur objects to.

---

[42] See Daniel Boyarin's *Sephardi Speculation: A Study in Methods of Talmudic Interpretation* (Jerusalem: Ben Zvi Institute, 1989).

[43] This is clear from the third of the causes that Maimonides says account for the difficulty in studying metaphysics: the length of the preliminary studies. *Guide* 49 (20), 73.

[44] Faur, 'Anti-Maimonidean Demons', 40–45.

[45] Menachem Kellner, 'An Ante-Mundane Torah – A Maimonidean Study', *Daʼat* 61 (2007).

[46] For examples see chapter four of Kellner's *Maimonides on the Decline of the Generations and the Nature of Rabbinic Authority* (Albany: State University of New York Press, 1996).

[47] Abot 3, 17.

[48] Kellner, 'An Ante-Mundane Torah?', 91.

[49] See his 'One Dimensional Jew, Zero Dimensional Judaism', *Annual of Rabbinic Judaism* 2 (1999).

Among the targets of both Kellner's and Faur's work are anti-rationalist world-views. According to Kellner they insist on not paying attention to universal reason and science but, rather, supporting opinions by looking for them in traditional sources. According to Faur they undermine the nature of the traditional sources by elevating the role of an individual's intuition in halakhic rulings above more normative methods of decision making, methods that rely upon discussion intelligible to other sages and posqim rather than on an individual's whim. In both cases the authority is sought in something not in principle universally accessible. Similarly, the difference between Maimonides, on the one hand, and the anti-Maimonideans, on the other, lies according to both scholars in the tools with which one ought to interpret the tradition: should they be norms intelligible to other trained wise people, and therefore, in principle, universal, as Maimonides and his followers would claim, or should tradition be filtered through the few who are uniquely qualified to interpret it, a qualification deriving solely from their 'intuitive' ability to converse, or somehow communicate, with a supernatural realm?[50]

Different attitudes towards reasoned debate go a long way to explaining the difference between the positions of the Maimonideans and their opponents. Those who opposed philosophy considered it to be an expression of human arrogance, since it presumes to be able to explain things for which explanations ought not to be sought. For its supporters, on the other hand, philosophy is the model of humility and patience, so long as its limits are recognised. This is the humility and patience with which Maimonides asks his readers to approach the *Guide* when he tells them they should constantly read the treatise. The difference between the philosophers' account of philosophy's scope and purpose, on the one hand, and the account of the opponents of philosophy, on the other, is crucial. Indeed, whether or not Maimonides' own account of Aristotle is accurate, he presents Aristotle in a similar way, as an honest seeker after truth who was perfectly aware of his own intellectual limitations and the limitations of his methodology. Maimonides attributes his differences of opinion to the fact that Aristotle is not part of the Abrahamic prophetic tradition, not to an intellectual hubris.[51] The philosophers try to carry out a committed search for truth, a search which takes place in the margins, even though it has been marginalised. Such a search requires one to think honestly and charitably about ideas.

The nature of the *Guide* is such that understanding it requires one to interact and to think creatively. From this perspective, the teacher – Maimonides – would be more concerned that the pupils – the readers of the *Guide* – think matters through for themselves rather than accept Maimonides' 'true' opinion. Maimonides is less concerned with revealing his 'hidden' view to the elite while concealing it from the vulgar than with encouraging the student to develop and work out the truth. That is why the *Guide* is written in a way that is so challenging to read. It is not simple because it is a *Guide* to a way of thought, and even a way of life, that is not simple. Without effort on the part of those who undertake the journey, there can be no journey. The ability to inhabit the margins is crucial. As a way of life it is creative and

---

[50] According to Kellner, Maimonides battled against a majority view and had very little success; his opponents remain in the majority. Indeed, Kellner believes that Maimonides unwittingly strengthened them as he explains in *Maimonides' Confrontation with Mysticism* (Oxford: The Littman Library of Jewish Civilization, 2006). According to Faur, he and, more importantly, his methods were marginalised because ideas taken from popular religion became authoritative.

[51] During the course of several chapters in which he argues that Aristotle was aware of the weaknesses of this own position, Maimonides claims the support of Moses and Abraham. See, for example, *Guide* 225 (8), 322.

dynamic; it is uncertain and therefore challenges any absolutes and idolatry. According to Faur, this understanding represents also an authentic way by which one ought to live Jewish texts.[52] When taken in such a way Maimonides' *Guide* points towards the conclusion that those who consider philosophy alien to Judaism because of its universal nature fail to distinguish between unqualified universal norms, and such norms as accessed by someone from within a living tradition. Although one gains access to universal norms through a particular gateway, they are nonetheless universal. For in fact, anyone's access can only come through a tradition in which she is steeped, and with which she contends in a constructive manner. The model of the *Guide* shows how struggling and growing in conversation with one's tradition can illuminate universal norms as well.

BIBLIOGRAPHY

Altmann, Alexander, 'Essence and Existence in Maimonides' in Buijs, ed., *Maimonides: A Collection of Critical Essays* (Notre Dame: University of Notre Dame Press, 1988).

Barnes, Jonathan ed., *The Complete Works of Aristotle: the revised Oxford translation* (Princeton: Princeton University Press, 1984).

Baneth, David, ed., *Letters of Maimonides* (Jerusalem: Mekize Nirdamim, 1946).

Berkovits, Eliezer, *Not in Heaven: The Nature and Function of Halakha* (New York: KTAV, 1983).

Boyarin, Daniel, *Sephardi Speculation: A Study in Methods of Talmudic Interpretation* (Jerusalem: Ben Zvi Institute, 1989).

Cole, Peter, *The Dream of the Poem: Hebrew Poetry from Muslim and Christian Spain* (Princeton and Oxford: Princeton University Press, 2007).

Davidson, Herbert, *Moses Maimonides: The Man and his Works* (New York: Oxford University Press, 2005).

Dobbs-Weinstein, Idit, 'The Maimonidean Controversy', *History of Jewish Philosophy* (London: Routledge, 1997).

Dubois, Marcel, *Temps et l'instant Selon Aristote* (Paris: Desclée de Brouwer, 1967).

Faur, Jose, 'Anti-Maimonidean Demons', *Review of Rabbinic Judaism* 6 (2003).

Faur, Jose, 'On Cultural Intimidation and other *Miscellanea*: Bar Sheshakh vs. Raba', *Review of Rabbinic Judaism* 5 (2002).

Faur, Jose, 'One Dimensional Jew, Zero Dimensional Judaism', *Annual of Rabbinic Judaism* 2 (1999).

Faur, Jose, *Homo Mysticus: A Guide to Maimonides' Guide for the Perplexed* (New York: Syracuse University Press, 1998).

Feldman, Seymour, *Philosophy in a time of Crisis: Don Isaac Abravanel, Defender of the Faith* (London and New York: RoutledgeCurzon, 2003).

Frank, Richard, *Creation and the Cosmic System: Al-Ghazâlî & Avicenna* (Heidelberg: Carl Winter, 1992).

Ghazāli, *The Incoherence of the Philosophers* A parallel English-Arabic text translated, introduced and annotated by Michael E. Marmura (Provo, Utah: Brigham Young University Press, 1997).

Gutas, Dimitri, 'The Study of Arabic Philosophy in the Twentieth Century: An Essay on the Historiography of Arabic Philosophy', *British Journal of Middle Eastern Studies* 29 (2002).

Kellner, Menachem, 'An Ante-Mundane Torah? – A Maimonidean Study', in *Da'at* 61 (2007).

---

[52] As well as the pieces mentioned above, see his 'On Cultural Intimidation and other *Miscellanea*: Bar Sheshakh vs. Raba', *Review of Rabbinic Judaism* 5 (2002).

Kellner, Menachem, *Maimonides' Confrontation with Mysticism* (Oxford: The Littman Library of Jewish Civilization, 2006).

Kellner, Menachem, *Maimonides on the Decline of the Generations and the Nature of Rabbinic Authority* (Albany: State University of New York Press, 1996).

Kraemer, Joel, 'How (not) to read the Guide of the Perplexed', *Jerusalem Studies in Arabic and Islam* 32 (2006).

Kraemer, Joel, 'Moses Maimonides: An Intellectual Portrait', *The Cambridge Companion to Maimonides* (Cambridge: Cambridge University Library, 2005).

Langermann, Tzvi, 'Maimonides' Repudiation of Astrology', *Maimonidean Studies* 2 (1991).

Maimonides, *Dalālat al-Ḥā'irīn* edited by Solomon Munk (Jerusalem: Azriel, 1929).

Maimonides, *The Guide of the Perplexed* translated by Shlomo Pines (Chicago: Chicago University Press, 1963).

Maimonidis *More Nebuchim (Doctor Perplexorum) ex versione Samuelis Tibbonidae cum commentariis Ephodaei, Schemtob, Ibn Crescas, nec non Don Isaci Abravanel asjectis summariis et indicibus* (Berlin: Adolf Cohn Verlag und Antiquariat, 1875).

Moosa, Ebrahim, *Ghazālī and the Poetics of Imagination* (Chapel Hill: The University of North Carolina Press, 2005).

Seeskin, Kenneth, *Maimonides: A Guide for Today's Perplexed* (West Orange: Behrman House, 1991).

Shapiro, Marc, *The Limits of Orthodox Theology: Maimonides' Thirteen Principles Reappraised* (Oxford, Portland Oregon: The Littman Library of Jewish Civilization, 2004).

Shem Tov ibn Shem Tov, *Sefer Emunot* (Ferrara: Abraham ibn Ushki, 1556).

Smith, Steven, *Reading Leo Strauss* (Chicago and London: The University of Chicago Press, 2006).

Touati, Charles, 'Le problème de l'inerrance prophétique dans la théologie juive du Moyen Age', *Revue de L'Histoire des Religions* 174 (1968).

Walbridge, John, *The Leaven of the Ancients: Suhrawardi and the Heritage of the Greeks* (Albany: State University of New York Press, 2000).

THEORETICAL APPROACHES TO DEFINING JEWISH IDENTITY, AND THE CASE OF FELIX MENDELSSOHN

Daniel R. Langton*

It is possible to outline two ways of approaching the subject of Felix Mendelssohn's Jewishness in relation to his oratorio *St Paul*. Firstly, one can consider certain theoretical considerations that emerge from the field of Jewish Cultural Studies in relation to complex Jewish identity in the modern world. In the light of these considerations, it will be suggested that the *St Paul* libretto shows the impact of his Jewish heritage and, in fact, demonstrates nicely the messy kind of Jewish self-consciousness that is often of greatest interest to scholars in the field. Secondly, one can consider the context of Jewish approaches to the apostle Paul. Here it will be suggested that Mendelssohn's oratorio can be seen to function in a very similar way insofar as he seems to blur the boundary between Judaism and Christianity.

Felix Mendelssohn (1809–1847) was a grandson of the famous Jewish Enlightenment philosopher, Moses Mendelssohn, and a son of the banker, Abraham Mendelssohn, who had him baptised as a seven year-old. A musical child prodigy who has been frequently compared to Mozart, Felix went on to become a renowned conductor and composer whose work mediated between the Classical and Romantic traditions.[1] Among the many symphonies, concertos, oratorios, piano and chamber music that he wrote in his short lifetime, two of his most famous works were the oratorios *Elijah* (1846) and, of greatest interest here, *St. Paul* (1836).[2]

A passionate debate currently rages amongst scholars as to whether Felix defined himself Jewishly or not. No-one disputes that he was a proud German and a sincere Christian. Rather, the focus of the debate is how important, if at all, Felix's Jewish heritage was to his religious worldview and, by extension, to his work. The history of this controversy is long and not a little sordid. An influential anti-Semitic attack by Wagner in 1850, shortly after Felix's death, had sought to marginalise his works by reference to their perceived Jewish characteristics[3] and the Nazis took up this theme and went on to ban performances of his

* Professor of the History of Jewish-Christian Relations, University of Manchester. Email: daniel.langton@ manchester.ac.uk This essay has appeared in modified version in Daniel R. Langton, 'Felix Mendelssohn's Oratorio St. Paul and the Question of Self-Identity', *Journal of Jewish Identities* 1/1 (2008) and in the same author's *The Apostle Paul in the Jewish Imagination* (Cambridge: Cambridge University Press, 2010).

[1] For a comprehensive biographical study, see R. Larry Todd, *Mendelssohn: A Life in Music* (Oxford: Oxford University Press, 2003).

[2] The first German edition was Felix Mendelssohn-Bartholdy, *Paulus* (Bonn: N. Simrock, 1836). The first English edition was Felix Mendelssohn, *St. Paul* (Birmingham: 1837).

[3] Wagner published 'Das Judenthum in der Musik', *Neue Zeitschrift für Musik* (Leipzig: 1850) under a pseudonym. He describes Mendelssohn's music as 'vague, fantastic shadow-forms', having already explained that '[a]lthough the peculiarities of the Jewish mode of speaking and singing come out the most glaringly in the commoner class of Jew, who has remained faithful to his fathers' stock, and though the cultured son of Jewry takes untold pains to strip them off, nevertheless they shew an impertinent obstinacy in cleaving to him.' Richard Wagner, *Judaism in Music and other Writings*, trans. W. Ashton Ellis (London: University of Nebraska Press, 1995), 89, 96.

music from 1938. In a classic study by Werner in 1963, the negative value-judgment of Felix's Jewishness was reversed and a portrayal of a great musician was offered that stressed Jewish influences and pride in his Jewish heritage.[4] However, recent research by Sposato has discredited much of Werner's presentation, showing that he modified the wording of key correspondence in making his case. Sposato argues instead that Felix saw himself as 'enlightened, rationalist, and, in short, a typical German *Neuchrist*'[5] as Jewish converts to Christianity were called, brought up and baptised as a Protestant and eventually becoming a follower of the highly influential Reformed theologian Friedrich Schleiermacher (1768–1834),[6] with no documented interest in his Jewish ancestry. Certainly, evidence to the contrary is hard to come by and appears to amount to a report that Felix once commented on the irony that he, as a 'Jew-boy', had brought about a revival of the church composer J.S. Bach.[7] Nevertheless, other scholars, including Botstein, Steinberg and Todd, while accepting Sposato's demolition of Werner's account, continue to regard Felix's Jewish background as important for making sense of the man and his music. All agree that in nineteenth-century German society, Felix could not have avoided his Jewishness even if he had so desired.[8] But while Sposato stresses that he chose not to *define* himself as such, the others remain convinced of the importance of his Jewish heritage for understanding him.[9] In particular, Botstein argues that Felix's lifework was the completion of a 'syncretic' project to 'universalise Judaism', a project first began with his grandfather Moses Mendelssohn.[10] In fact, there is not as much distance between the two camps as appears at first sight. Sposato's meticulous study is certainly prepared to acknowledge a development in Felix's writing which, by the end of his life, had arrived at what is described as a 'strategy of dual

---

[4] Eric Werner, *A New Image of the Composer and his Age*, trans. Dika Newlin (New York: Collier-Macmillan, 1963).

[5] Jeffrey S. Sposato, 'Creative Writing: The [Self-] Identification of Mendelssohn as a Jew', *The Musical Quarterly* 82:1 (Spring 1998), 192.

[6] The distinction between the Reformed (Calvinist) and Lutheran churches in Prussia at the time had mainly to do with liturgy. Felix proclaimed himself 'a follower of Schleiermacher' in 1830 in a letter to his friend Julius Schubring, himself a disciple of the theologian who sought to reconcile Lutheran and Reformed theology; he also cultivated a personal friendship with Schleiermacher. Jeffrey Sposato, *The Price of Assimilation: Felix Mendelssohn and the Nineteenth-Century Anti-Semitic Tradition* (Oxford: Oxford University Press, 2006), 48, 186n39.

[7] 'To think that it must be a comic-actor and a Jew-boy [Judenjunge] who brings back to the people the greatest Christian musical work!' Eduard Devrient, *Meine Erinnerungen an Felix Mendelssohn* or *My Memories of Felix Mendelssohn* (Leipzig: J.J. Weber, 1872), 62.

[8] Spozato himself observes, 'That Mendelssohn identified in part as Jewish is beyond question. How could he not have, with queens, princes, fellow musicians, and friends all, to a greater or lesser extent, seeing him as such?' but he argues forcefully that this was of little or no real consequence. Sposato, *The Price of Assimilation*, 14.

[9] Steinberg responds directly to Sposato's categorization of Mendelssohn by asserting that 'Felix Mendelssohn's cultural moment and biographical formation cannot be understood as those of a 'typical *Neuchrist*' but rather as a paradigm of a multicultural and uncertain moment in German Jewish history that was available only to the Biedermeier generation, that is, the generation of 1815–1848. The assertion that Mendelssohn should be considered a Protestant rather than Jew simply replaces one conceptually and historically inadequate label with another.' Michael P. Steinberg, 'Mendelssohn's Music and German-Jewish Culture: An Intervention', *The Musical Quarterly* 83:1 (Spring 1999), 32. Todd draws upon both Botstein and Sposato, concluding 'we must begin to realize the significance of the composer's own project of assimilation, of finding ground between his adopted faith and the rationalist Judaism of his grandfather, Moses Mendelssohn.' Todd, *Mendelssohn: A Life in Music*, xxviii.

[10] Writing before Sposato, Botstein's argument (which remains unchanged) was that '[Felix] Mendelssohn was syncretic, not sectarian. His Christian faith focused on the extent to which Christianity was a universalization of Judaism.' Leon Botstein 'The Aesthetics of Assimilation and Affirmation: Reconstructing the Career of Felix Mendelssohn' in R. Larry Todd, ed., *Mendelssohn and His World* (Princeton: Princeton University Press, 1991), 23.

perspective', that is, 'an attempt to reconcile his Christian faith and his Jewish heritage.'[11] It is agreed, then, that Felix's shifting attitude towards Jews and his consciousness of both Jewish and Christian perspectives – and its implications for his self-understanding – can be traced in his works. For those interested in complex Jewish identity, whatever the precise label given, his oratorio about the Apostle to the Gentiles has some particularly useful insights to offer.

When it comes to defining Jewish identity or 'Jewishness' in a systematic way, one's assumptions play a major role. One tendency, not uncommon among theologians, is to essentialize by classifying people and phenomena as Jewish only in so far as they conform to an assumed essence of a normative Jewishness. This essence may or may not be related to theologically derived criteria such as matrilineal decent, conversion to a particular tradition or set of beliefs, adherence to a certain body of law, a role in salvation history, or to non-theological criteria such as racial, national or cultural characteristics. From this perspective, responsibility for determining Jewish authenticity rests entirely with the observer, irrespective of whether his views originate from within the community or from outside. For the essentialist, anything or anyone who does not correspond to the given definition is to be excluded as marginal at best and deviant at worst. One might imagine a core of authenticity surrounded by concentric circles of ever decreasing legitimacy. The problem, of course, is that observers do not agree on what exactly constitutes the core of authenticity. Whichever definition is to be regarded as authoritative depends upon one's existing biases. Furthermore, proponents of essentialism do not tend to recognise the historically-conditioned nature of such definitions and often assume that the characteristics of Jewish authenticity have remained fundamentally unchanged down through the ages.[12]

An alternative method of categorization is that of 'self-definition', the approved method for many social scientists and historians. This non-essentialist approach does not pre-determine the outer limits of Jewishness and so 'deviancy' or 'marginality' are terms free of negative connotations. The inclusion of those who define themselves Jewishly can lead to political controversies, such as the acceptance of Messianic Jews despite their dismissal as Christians-by-another-name by a broad spectrum of the Jewish community. But the advantage of a self-definitional approach is that it largely frees the observer from the responsibility for selection and minimises the projection onto the subject of his own ideological biases. For some, 'self-definition' implies that the individual defines himself *primarily* in Jewish terms, but this need not be the case. Arguably, an individual can possess a self-image that includes a Jewish *component*, however he defines it. This is an important point, especially in the context of intercultural studies which take for granted overlapping or hierarchical identities. Nor should one forget that an individual's self-image evolves and transforms in real time and changes according to social context. The self-definitional

---

[11] Sposato suggests that a changing attitude towards Jews is apparent from the time of Felix's revival of the St. Matthew Passion in 1829, through the libretto drafted for A.B. Marx's *Mose* in 1833 and the oratorios of *St. Paul* (1836), *Elijah* (1846), and *Christ* (1847). The new attitude revealed in the last two works was 'one no longer fuelled by a need to demonize the Jews in order to prove the sincerity of his Christian faith.' Sposato, *The Price of Assimilation*, 178–179.

[12] For a powerful critique of the essentializing tendency, see Laurence J. Silberstein, *Mapping Jewish Identities* (New York: New York University Press, 2000).

approach is commonly used because it attempts to accommodate the complex, shifting reality of Jewish identity.[13]

Unfortunately, 'self-definition' excludes many who do not appear to see themselves in Jewish terms and yet who live lives and produce works that strike the sensitive observer as inexplicable without reference to a Jewish dimension of some sort. Celebrated examples include the seventeenth-century philosopher Baruch Spinoza and, of course, Felix Mendelssohn. A work of monumental Jewish scholarship such as the *Encyclopaedia Judaica* will include such problematic individuals because of its working principle that 'anyone born a Jew' is qualified for inclusion, even if he later converted or disassociated himself from Jewish life, as are individuals born of only one Jewish parent who are 'sufficiently distinguished.[14] But no theoretical justification is offered for this approach and it appears to be premised upon unacknowledged essentialist assumptions of a theological and / or racial kind. Is it possible to qualify the self-definitional method, so that a more nuanced treatment of such individuals can be offered that avoids the common essentialist definitions?

The key question, surely, is whether a significant part of an individual's worldview is best explained in terms of his self-identification at some level as a Jew, and whether the failure to take this dimension seriously would result in an impoverished understanding of his life and work. (For present purposes, it does not matter whether the individual's perception of Jewishness or Judaism is real or imagined). For those Jews who later convert to Christianity or who try to disassociate from Jewish life in general, breaking the psychological ties of association is very difficult, if not impossible. This is especially true for those living in the modern period, when the authority of the Church, and its belief in the transformative power of baptism, was losing ground to the natural sciences and the assumption of eternal and fixed species. Mendelssohn, for example, would have been well aware that his contemporaries continued to see in him an indelible trace of Jewishness and, at some level at least, he must have internalised this social reality. One should be wary of underestimating the impact of this kind of 'intersubjective' assessment of Jewishness.[15] To put it another way, it might be possible to expand the self-definitional approach to include those born Jews who, after leaving the community, continue to self-identify as Jews on some level. The problem is how an observer can know whether the individual so identifies if this association is not articulated explicitly. Arguably, Mendelssohn should be included under the self-definitional approach if a case can be made that an awareness of his identification as a Jew at some level contributes in a significant sense to an understanding of his composition, in this case, the oratorio

---

[13] For a survey of the changing understandings of Jewishness, especially in the ancient world, see Shaye J.D. Cohen, *The Beginnings of Jewishness: Boundaries, Varieties, Uncertainties* (Berkley: University of California Press, 1999).

[14] In their introduction the editors write, 'In certain biographical entries a problem was to determine who was a Jew. The first principle adopted was that anyone born a Jew qualified for inclusion, even if he or she had subsequently converted or otherwise dissociated himself from Jewish life (where these facts are known, they are stated). The second principle was that a person with one Jewish parent would qualify for inclusion (with the relevant information stated) if he or she were sufficiently distinguished. A person whose Jewish origins were more remote would only be the subject of an entry in very unusual cases. However, a more generous attitude was taken in the case of Marranos, in view of the special circumstances surrounding their history.' Geoffrey Wigoder and Fern Seckbach, 'Editor's Introduction', *Encyclopaedia Judaica*, 7.

[15] In this vein Krausz has argued that 'Jewishness is understood as *a set of characteristic positions in which certain people are cast or ascribed – by themselves and by others.*' Michael Krausz, 'On Being Jewish' in David Theo Goldberg and Michael Krausz, eds., *Jewish Identity* (Philadelphia: Temple University Press, 1993), 266.

St Paul. Consequentially, both the subject and the observer must share the responsibility for establishing 'self-definition' because however much depends upon the subject's assumptions, attitudes, value-judgments and ideas, just as much hangs on the observer's ability to uncover and interpret them in their historical context. One can make a useful distinction in this regard between essentialist, ahistorical characteristics of Jewishness and historically- and culturally-determined characteristics of what constitutes Jewishness.[16] What follows, then, is an attempt to connect Mendelssohn's work to a self-conscious accommodation with his Jewish heritage. It is an attempt to offer a plausible reading of his carefully edited libretto as an expression of religious sentiment that was by no means entirely hostile to Judaism *as he conceived it at that time*, and which allowed him to identity with it, at some level.

Let us begin with a brief overview of the intellectual influences within Felix's family for the purpose of establishing the foundations of his own religious constitution. One might be tempted to begin with his grandfather, Moses Mendelssohn (1729–1786),[17] whose writings can be seen as an attempt to relate eighteenth-century rationality and theism. After all, Felix was instrumental, at least at an initial stage, in having Moses' collected works published only four years after the completion of *St. Paul*.[18] The book that made Moses' reputation, *Phaedon* (1767), was a discussion of immortality which drew heavily upon natural theology and assumed the universality of rational thought.[19] Felix read this extended commentary of Plato's treatise in 1831, only a year before work began on the *St. Paul* oratorio.[20] If Felix had also read Moses' classic study, *Jerusalem or On Religious Power and Judaism* (1783), which also featured a deist-like vision of a God who reveals his purposes and ethical demands through the natural world and by means of a common access to reason,[21] then this would have important implications for his

---

[16] Krausz maintains that one can 'distinguish between essentialism – the doctrine that there are ahistorically fixed conditions for a thing to be that thing – from what, at particular moments in historical evolution, are taken to be necessary conditions for a thing to be a thing.' Krausz, 'On Being Jewish', 267.

[17] Botstein is among those who would do so. 'Felix Mendelssohn's advocacy of his grandfather's work is certainly positive evidence of his connection to being Jewish. A revival of or an increase in awareness of his grandfather's writings by definition had to invoke a visible affirmation of Felix's Jewish heritage... Felix's knowledge of and lifelong admiration for Moses Mendelssohn's work was nontrivial.' Leon Botstein, 'Mendelssohn and the Jews', *The Musical Quarterly* 82:1 (Spring 1998), 212.

[18] It is, however, important not to over-estimate Felix's role in this. He was approached to assist with the publication of Moses Mendelssohn's works in 1840, but it was his uncle, Joseph, and Joseph's son Benjamin, who were actually responsible for bringing this product to a successful conclusion. Todd, *Mendelssohn: A Life in Music*, 16–17.

[19] '[T]he endowments he [man] possesses of body and mind, he knows to be the gift of the all-good Father. All beauties, all harmony, goodness, wisdom, providence, ways and means, which he has acknowledged hitherto in the visible and invisible world, he considers as thoughts of the Almighty, which are given him to read in the book of creation, in order to advance him to a higher perfection... [W]e fulfil the views of the supreme bring on earth by developing our intellectual capacities... In our eyes the world of moral beings speaks the perfection of its author, as strongly as the world of nature.' Moses Mendelssohn, *Phaedon or the Death of Socrates* (London: J. Cooper, 1789), 174–175, 181, 197. German original: Moses Mendelssohn, *Phaedon oder über die Unsterblichkeit der Seele in drey Gesprächen* (Berlin: Stettin, 1767). In an appendix to the third edition, Moses goes so far as to suggest that 'A friend of reason, such as he [Socrates] was, would certainly have gratefully accepted from other philosophers that part of their doctrine which was based on reason, no matter what country or religious party they otherwise belonged to. Where rational truths are concerned, one can agree with anyone, and nevertheless find many things untrustworthy which he accepts on faith.'

[20] Todd, *Mendelssohn: A Life in Music*, 244.

[21] In *Jerusalem* Moses wrote 'It is true that I recognize no eternal truths other than those that are not merely comprehensible to human reason but can also be demonstrated and verified by human powers... I consider this an essential point of the Jewish religion and believe that this doctrine constitutes a characteristic difference between it and the Christian one... Eternal truths... insofar as they are useful for men's salvation and felicity, are taught by God

conception of the Jewish religion. However, with the exception of *Phaedon* there is no direct evidence that Felix actually read Moses' works (as Sposato points out), and while it is difficult to imagine that his famous grandfather's writings and ideas were of no interest to the cultivated, intellectual household in which Felix was brought up, one must be cautious about attributing to them too great an influence.[22] Firmer ground is found with Felix's father, Abraham Mendelssohn-Bartholdy (1776–1835), whom Felix deeply respected and from whom he sought approval throughout his life. The views of the father are important for what they tell us about the kind of religious environment in which the son was actually raised. In common with other assimilationist Jews of his day, Abraham was attracted to a rationalist perspective and his religious worldview was wary of theism of any sort. While he rejected Judaism he did not offer a ringing endorsement of Christianity, either, as he made clear in several letters to his children. In 1820, at around the time of the confirmation of Felix's sister, Fanny, Abraham discussed his conception of religion at some length.[23] For Abraham the label 'Christian' was a matter of convenience, an appellation adopted for society's sake, and his real concern for his daughter was for her to find happiness in an ethical, dutiful life. Ultimately, the label made little difference for, as he put it elsewhere, 'There are in all religions only one God, one virtue, one truth, one happiness.'[24] In a letter to Felix in 1829,[25] there is again a clear sense of grudging

---

in a manner more appropriate to the Deity; not by sounds or written characters, which are comprehensible here and there, to this or that individual, but through creation itself, and its internal relations, which are legible and comprehensible to all men. Nor does He confirm them by miracles... but He awakens the mind, which He has created, and gives it an opportunity to observe the relations of things, to observe itself, and to become convinced of the truths which it is destined to understand here below.' Moses Mendelssohn, *Jerusalem or On Religious Power and Judaism*, trans. by Allan Arkush (New England: Brandeis, 1983), 89, 93. German original: Moses Mendelssohn, *Jerusalem oder über religiöse Macht und Judentum* (Berlin: Maurer, 1783). Moses also believed that the revealed Law could likewise be explained in terms of a rational purpose, and could be regarded as 'the foundation for the national cohesion.' Mendelssohn, *Jerusalem*, 126–128.

[22] Sposato notes that in a letter dated February 1842 Felix wrote that he did not possess 'a single page of his [Moses'] writing', which he reads as indicative of a lack of interest. Sposato, *The Price of Assimilation*, 36.

[23] 'Does God exist? What is God? Is He part of ourselves, and does He continue to live after the other part has ceased to be? And where? And how? All this I do not know, and therefore I have never taught you anything about it. But I know that there exists in me and in you and in all human beings an everlasting inclination towards all that is good, true and right, and a conscience which warns and guides us when we go astray. I know it, I believe it, I live in this faith, and this is my religion... This is all I can tell you about religion, all I know about it; but this will remain true, as long as one man will exist in the creation, as it has been true since the first man was created. The outward form of religion your teacher has given you is historical, and changeable like all human ordinances. Some thousands of years ago the Jewish form was the reigning one, then the heathen form, and now it is the Christian... We have educated you and your brothers and sister in the Christian faith, because it is the creed of most civilized people, and contains nothing that can lead you away from what is good, and much that guides you to love, obedience, tolerance, and resignation... By pronouncing your confession of faith you have fulfilled the claims of *society* on you, and obtained the *name* of a Christian. Now be what your duty as a human being demands of you, *true, faithful, good*; obedient and devoted till death to your mother, and I may also say to your father, unremittingly attentive to the voice of your conscience,... and you will gain the highest happiness that is to be found on earth, harmony and contentedness with yourself.' Letter from Abraham Mendelssohn to Fanny Mendelssohn (1820) reproduced in Sebastian Hensel, *The Mendelssohn Family*, trans. by Carl Klingemann, second edition (New York: Harper, 1882), 1:79–80.

[24] Letter from Abraham Mendelssohn to Fanny Mendelssohn (1819) reproduced in S. Hensel, *The Mendelssohn Family*, 1:77.

[25] 'I had learned, and until my last breath will never forget, that the truth is one and eternal; its forms, however, are many and transitory; and so I raised you, to the extent that the constitution under which we then lived permitted it, free from any religious form, which I wished to leave you to your own convictions, should they demand it, or to your choice, based on considerations of convenience. That was not to be, however, and I had to choose for you. Given the scant value I place on all [religious] forms, it goes without saying that I felt no inner calling to choose for you the Jewish, the most obsolete, corrupt, and pointless of them [all]. So I raised you in the Christian, the purer

necessity in raising his children as Christians, as dictated by the bigotry of wider society,[26] even if an outmoded Judaism, as he saw it, was entirely out of the question. For Abraham, 'religion' was, in essence, a universal ethic towards which humankind is progressing that had once been clothed in the apparel of Judaism and was now wrapped in the garments of Christianity. It was a historical view of religion that simultaneously linked Judaism and Christianity but went beyond them, and, arguably, Abraham did not see his conversion (six years after his son's baptism) or change of name (to Mendelssohn-Bartholdy) as a rejection of Moses Mendelssohn's core values, but rather as a continuation or extension of them, the fulfilment of an ideological trajectory; for him, the Mendelssohn name symbolized 'Judaism in transition'.[27] This schema of a transitional relation between Judaism and Christianity is worth noting because, as will become clear, it was implicit in Felix's composition of *St. Paul*, despite the fact that the connection was minimised by the Lutheran and Reformed theologies with which he publicly associated himself.

Let us restrict ourselves to two general questions. What themes can be derived from the texts selected by Felix? And what should be made of the materials and corresponding themes that he chose *not* to include?

Firstly, the materials chosen. Many commentators, both in Felix's day and afterwards, have complained about the amount of space devoted to the martyrdom of Stephen.[28] After all, the dramatic potential for Saul, such as it is, lies in his (very marginal) involvement in the

---

[form] accepted by the majority of civilised people, and also confessed the same for myself, because I had to do myself what I recognized as best for you.' Letter from Abraham Mendelssohn to Felix Mendelssohn (1829). M. Schneider, *Mendelssohn oder Bartholdy?* (Basel: Internationale Felix-Mendelssohn-Gesellschaft, 1962), 18–19, cited in Sposato, *The Price of Assimilation*, 16.

[26] Abraham discussed the matter with his wife's brother, who had changed his name from Salomon to Bartholdy, and who apparently convinced him to do likewise in correspondence: 'You say you owe it to the memory of your father [to remain a Jew] – do you think you have done anything evil by giving your children the religion which you consider the best one *for them*? Rather it is an act of homage which you and I and all of us owe to Moses Mendelssohn's efforts in the interests of true Enlightenment... A man can remain loyal to an oppressed, persecuted religion; he can impose it on his children as a candidature for a lifelong martyrdom – *as long as he thinks that it alone will bring salvation*. But as soon as he no longer believes that, it is barbarism to do anything of the kind.' Letter to Abraham Mendelssohn (undated) reproduced in S. Hensel, *The Mendelssohn Family*, 1:75.

[27] Abraham wrote to Felix, 'My father felt that the name Moses den Mendel Dessau would handicap him in gaining the needed access to those who had the better education at their disposal. Without any fear that his own father would take offence, my father assumed the name Mendelssohn. The change, though a small one, was decisive. As Mendelssohn, he became irrevocably detached from an entire class, the best of whom he raised to his own level. By that name he identified himself with another group. Through the influence which, ever growing, persists to this day, the name Mendelssohn acquired great authority and a significance which defies extinction. This, considering that you were reared a Christian, you can hardly understand. A Christian Mendelssohn is an impossibility. A Christian Mendelssohn the world would never recognise. Nor should there be a Christian Mendelssohn; for my father himself did not want to be a Christian. "Mendelssohn" does and always will stand for a Judaism in transition, when Judaism, just because it is seeking to transmute itself spiritually, clings to its ancient form all the more stubbornly and tenaciously, by way of protest against the novel form that so arrogantly and tyrannically declared itself to be the one and only path to the good.' Letter from Abraham Mendelssohn to Felix Mendelssohn (8 July 1829) reproduced in Michael P. Steinberg, 'Mendelssohn's Music and German-Jewish Culture: An Intervention', *The Musical Quarterly* 83:1 (Spring 1999), 37–38.

[28] In fact even his father, Abraham, complained, but Felix's polite reply (included within a letter to his sister) does not offer any explanation. 'The non-appearance of St. Paul at the stoning of Stephen is certainly a blemish, and I could easily alter the passage in itself; but I could find absolutely no mode of introducing him at the time, and no words from him to utter in accordance with the Scriptural narrative; therefore it seemed to me more expedient to follow the biblical account, and to make Stephen appear alone. I think, however, that your other censure is obviated by the music; for the recitative of Stephen, though the words are long, will not occupy more than two or three minutes, – or *including* all the choruses – till his death, about quarter of an hour.' Letter from Felix Mendelssohn to Rebecca Dirichlet (23 December 1834) reproduced in P. and C. Mendelssohn Bartholdy, eds., *Letters of Felix Mendelssohn Bartholdy*, 62–63.

murder of a Christian saint and his consequent inauguration as a persecutor of the new sect — and this might easily have been dealt with in fewer than the eleven sections it actually takes. However, one key theme to emerge is that of the contrast between the ideas of the Jews, whose religion was focused on the Law and Temple, and Stephen's more spiritual conception of the nature of their God as the creator of the natural world.[29] To begin with, Felix reproduces the testimony of the Jewish false witnesses, who shout 'We verily have heard him blaspheme against these holy places, and against the law' (Acts 6:14), and has 'the Jews' as a group express similar complaints.[30] In recounting the speech that Stephen made in response, about the rebellious history of the Hebrews, Felix is especially careful to include the passages in Acts which condemns them for idol worship[31] and where the importance of the Temple is denigrated, drawing attention instead to God's sovereignty over nature.[32] This key theme of God as Creator of the natural world is reinforced by the choice of the text for the first chorus of the oratorio, which exclaims, 'LORD, Thou alone art God; and Thine are the heavens, the earth and the mighty waters' (Acts 4:24). But Felix is not critical of the Jews alone. In a later episode in Lystra in which Paul is mistaken by pagans for a god after having performed a healing, a similar critique is made of *the Gentiles* who appear even more confused about the nature of God than had the Jews. Felix cites at length Paul's rebuke to the Gentiles' intention to sacrifice to and adore him as a god, which includes his warning that:

> you should turn away from all these vanities unto the ever living God, who made the outstretched heavens, the earth and the sea. As saith the Prophet: 'All your idols are but falsehood, and there is no breath in them. They are vanity, and the work of errors: in the time of their trouble they shall perish.' God dwelleth not in temples made with human hands. (Acts 14:15; Jeremiah 10:14,15; Acts 17:24)

Felix immediately follows this with Paul's question, 'For know you not that ye are His temple, and that the spirit of God dwelleth in you?.. For the temple of God is holy, which temple you are' (1 Corinthians 3:16,17).[33] As if to drive home the errors of the Jewish and pagan conceptions of deity, Felix has the Jews *and Gentiles* (who do not appear in the biblical text) come together to assault Paul in a joint chorus in section 38,

> This is Jehovah's temple. Ye children of Israel, help us. This is the man who teacheth all men, against the people, against this place, and also our holy law. We have heard him speak blasphemies against the law. He blasphemes God. Stone him. (Acts 21:28)

Thus Felix's editorial choices imply that Jew and Gentile alike have misunderstood the nature of God, and have set up idols, temples and laws as a result of their ignorance of the

---

[29] Sposato sees this critique of the Jewish obsession with the Law as evidence of anti-Semitism (which he prefers to the term 'anti-Judaic' in this context). Sposato, *The Price of Assimilation*, 10–11.

[30] Now this man [Stephen] ceaseth not to utter blasphemous words *against the law of Moses*, and also God... He hath said, and we have heard him, [that] Jesus of Nazareth He shall destroy all these *our holy places*, and *change all the laws and customs* which Moses delivered us. (Acts 6:11, 14).

[31] 'But they refused him [Moses] and would not obey his word, but thrust him from them, and sacrificed to senseless idols' (Acts 7:39–40).

[32] Solomon built Him an house; albeit the Most High God dwelleth not in temples which are made with hands; for heaven is His throne, and earth is but His footstool. Has not His hand made all these things? (Acts 7:47–48)

[33] This is followed by a chorus that confirms, 'But our God abideth in heaven: His will directeth all the world. We bow to only His decree, Who made the skies, the earth and sea' (Psalm 115:3).

true Creator of the Universe.[34] In contrast, Felix projects onto Paul (and Stephen) a deist-like admiration of the divine watchmaker, whose temple is to be found within man and who is properly worshipped through the spiritual appreciation of nature, as suggested by the paean of praise of God as the source of all knowledge that ends the first part of the oratorio.[35] What is of significance here is that Felix's particular understanding of Christianity as the path towards universal, rational enlightenment is by no means an obvious emphasis for a treatment of the life of St. Paul. To explain it, one might look to the foundational influence of his family. For while the kind of belief that characterises the oratorio has been described quite reasonably by Mercer-Taylor as 'an aesthetically blank lowest common denominator of the Christian community in the act of worship',[36] its assumptions concerning the rationalist underpinnings of religion and the shortcomings of its Jewish garb might as easily be said to have characterised the letters that Abraham Mendelssohn, the assimilated Jew, wrote to his children.[37] Likewise, in attempting to explain the theme of natural religion one is sorely tempted to consider the parallels to Moses Mendelssohn's famous adherence to a God who reveals his universal will to those who can detect it by observation of his creation, rather than find its source in Lutheran 'philo-Heathenism'[38] (a theory which does not take account of Felix's criticism of Gentiles, too). Of course, an interest in natural religion was very much in line with the wider German Enlightenment *zeitgeist*, and there is nothing remarkable about finding in the work of any composer of this time the rationalist emphasis characteristic of contemporary theology and philosophy of religion. *But the point is that, for a Mendelssohn at least, such ideas were not regarded as being in opposition to Judaism.* While the origin of such emphases must remain the subject of speculation, it is reasonable to suggest that Felix's conception of religion had been shaped by the Mendelssohn family's well-documented commitment to rational, universalist religion. In particular, his was a vision consistent with Abraham Mendelssohn's belief in a universal ethic that, in Paul's day, had progressed beyond the culturally determined limitations of paganism and *ancient* Judaism, and which would

---

[34] Sposato observes that, in the libretto, Gentiles respond more positively to Paul's missionary endeavours than do the Jews, and he suggests that this reflects a typical tendency of Lutheran and German Protestantism to glorify their Gentile heritage, which he calls 'philo-Heathenism'. Sposato, *The Price of Assimilation*, 92–94. But the reading of the libretto adopted here sees Mendelssohn equally critical of the shortcomings of Jewish legalism and Gentile idolatry.

[35] 'O great is the depth of the riches of wisdom and knowledge of the Father! How deep and unerring is He in His judgements! His ways are past our understanding. Sing to His glory forever more: Amen.' (Romans 11:33)

[36] Peter Mercer-Taylor, 'Rethinking Mendelssohn's Historicism: A Lesson from St Paul', *The Journal of Musicology* 15:2 (Spring 1997), 227.

[37] Botstein makes a similar observation regarding the source for Felix's rationalism. 'Insofar as Mendelssohn actually succeeded in integrating a Judaic element in the Protestant theology of the text of *St. Paul* Julius Schubring provided him, it was in the highlighting, through the choral numbers, of the abstract and rational substance of faith. Despite the prominence of the figure of Christ in *St. Paul* and the centrality of the conversion, it is the rational, ethical essence of faith that stands out... *St. Paul* represented Mendelssohn's musical-dramatic defence of the theological stance of Abraham Mendelssohn, who ultimately converted to Christianity himself. In *St. Paul*, baptism is the route to a rational enlightenment.' (Botstein overestimates the role of Schubring and exaggerates the prominence of Christ in the libretto). Leon Botstein, 'Songs without Words: Thoughts on Music, Theology, and the Role of the Jewish Question in the Work of Felix Mendelssohn', *The Musical Quarterly* 77:4 (Winter 1993), 574–575.

[38] Sposato attributes the theme of 'natural religion' to a German tradition that denigrated Judaism's significance for the Gentiles. In particular, he observes that both Luther and Schleiermacher had believed that God had revealed his law in nature, and therefore 'most of it... was also written into the hearts of the Gentiles before their conversion, thereby inviting Germans to view their ancestors not just as pre-Christian, but as proto-Christian, and therefore a people they could look back on with pride and respect.' *The Price of Assimilation*, 93–94.

undoubtedly move on again in time. Nor was it a view that necessarily did violence to Moses Mendelssohn's conception of Judaism as an essentially rational religion.

In addition to Felix's critique of Judaism's misplaced confidence in the Temple and the Law, and his portrayal of the rebellious character of the Hebrews as described in Stephen's speech, the oratorio provides further evidence of its author's negative attitude towards ancient Jewry.[39] Sposato has demonstrated how, through successive drafts of section 38, Felix eventually replaced the biblical account of Gentile opposition with that of an essentially Jewish opposition.[40] Furthermore, in the space of a few sections, Felix has the chorus of Hebrews twice chant Leviticus 24:16, in which the Law demands death for blasphemy.[41] And early in the second part, Felix focuses on the envy of the Jews at Paul's popularity with the masses, their arguments with him, and eventually their conspiracy to ambush and kill him. Furthermore, several choruses of Jews vigorously assert their rejection of the Saviour and their hostility to Paul and 'all deceivers'.[42] This negative portrayal of the Jews has been put down to the influence of Abraham Mendelssohn[43] or to the concerns of a *Neuchrist* to distance himself from the ancestral faith of which he was all too self-conscious. (As such, it is a phenomenon closely related to that of Jewish self-hatred, a topic of great interest within Jewish cultural studies). In any case, it represents a mechanism by which Felix can explain the apostle's momentous decision to turn from the Jews to the Gentiles, which is the point of sections 23–31. It concludes with his famous parting shot,

> Ye were chosen first to have the word of the Lord set before you; but, seeing that ye put it from you, and judge yourselves unworthy of the life everlasting, behold ye, we turn, even now, unto the Gentiles. (Act 13:46)

This leads us to two related themes which were more significant to Felix than the failings of the Jews, namely, (i) the universalization of the knowledge of the one true God and (ii) the sacrifice and martyrdom that made this possible, in his mind. The theme of sacrifice is very

---

[39] According to Sposato, Mendelssohn 'tried to distance himself from his [Jewish] heritage as much as possible... The editorial practices in his sacred music libretti also support this view of Mendelssohn, containing as they do numerous examples of the composer unnecessarily including anti-Semitic texts, such as that in the chorus 'His blood be upon us and our children' in his edition of *St. Matthew Passion* and those that add to his stereotypical depiction of the Jews as a law-obsessed people in *Paulus*.' Jeffrey S. Sposato, 'Creative Writing: The [Self-] Identification of Mendelssohn as a Jew', *The Musical Quarterly* 82:1 (Spring 1998), 204. For Sposato, this anti-Jewish strain is enough to demonstrate Felix's rejection of a Jewish identity, at least at the time of writing his *Paulus*. But this is to dismiss the complex, racial understanding of 'Jewishness' in nineteenth-century European Semitic discourse. Sposato himself observes that Felix's attitudes towards the Jews shifted throughout his lifetime, from which some might infer a lifelong struggle with a Jewish self-identification. Thus Felix's negative representation of the Jews in *Paulus* could be plausibly interpreted as an antagonistic posture adopted for complicated psychological and social reasons that reflect the complex reality of the Jewish conversion existence at that time and place, rather than simply as evidence that he did not self-identify as a Jew.

[40] Jeffrey S. Sposato, 'Mendelssohn, 'Paulus', and the Jews: A Response to Leon Botstein and Michael Steinberg', *The Musical Quarterly* 83:2 (Summer 1999), 284–288.

[41] The first Hebrew chorus is 'Take him away. For now the holy name of God he hath blasphemed; and he who blasphemes Him, he shall perish' while the second is 'Stone him to death. He blasphemes God; and who does so shall surely perish. Stone him to death.'

[42] One chorus sings 'Thus saith the Lord, 'I am the Lord, and beside me there is no Saviour'' (Isaiah 43:11) and another 'Is this he, who, in Jerusalem, destroyed all calling on that name which here he preacheth? May all deceivers ever be confounded! Force him away!' (Acts 9:21).

[43] 'By far the strongest influence on *Paulus*'s treatment of the Jews was [Felix] Mendelssohn's father... [D]uring Felix's youth, Abraham Mendelssohn continually encouraged his son to separate himself from his Jewish roots, both through instruction and by example.' Sposato, *The Price of Assimilation*, 90.

important and helps account for the structure of the oratorio and even for his interest in Paul in the first place. It is implicit in the death of Stephen himself, whose martyrdom was necessary in order to put Paul on the path to becoming the Apostle to the Gentiles, and whose story, as already noted, seems to have been given disproportionate attention.[44] The divinely ordained enlightenment of the Gentiles is a phenomenon referred to repeatedly throughout the work,[45] and is emphasised in the opening chorus of the second part, which pre-empts Paul's rejection of the Jews: 'The nations are now the Lord's'.[46] Felix's interest in the cost of universalization also explains the length of the conclusion, which is devoted to Paul's farewell to the elders of Ephesus. While not offering much in terms of drama, these final sections are replete with references to Paul's readiness to suffer death in the cause of taking the gospel message throughout the world.[47] Some commentators have complained at Felix's tendency toward sentimentalism, and, arguably, the final sections could be regarded as an over-indulgent expression of the pathos of Paul's life. Building a case for the influence of Christian influence, Sposato has seen here confirmation of his Christological concerns.[48] But it also ties together Moses Mendelssohn's emphasis on the universality of religious truth, and Abraham Mendelssohn's painful conviction of the necessity of severing his children's ties to the outmoded religious language of Judaism in favour of Christianity. There's no hard evidence, of course, and I may be quite wrong, but it is at least psychologically plausible that Felix's meditation (on the sacrifice necessary to achieve universal knowledge of the one true God) is the result of an acute awareness of what 'Judaism in transition' really means, at least in the experience of the Mendelssohn family.

---

[44] Felix also chooses to include the references in Stephen's speech relating the persecution and suffering of God's messengers: 'Which of the Prophets have not your fathers persecuted? And they have slain them which showed before the coming of Him, the Just one, with whose murder ye have here been stained' (Acts 7:52) and a similar gospel passage, 'Jerusalem, Jerusalem, thou that killest the Prophets, and stonest them which are sent unto thee' (Matthew 23:37).

[45] Texts that Felix uses to allude to the Gentiles' salvation include: Acts 4:26,29 ('And the kings of the earth took their stand and the rulers were gathered together against the Lord and against his Christ... And now, Lord, take note of their threats, and grant that Your bond-servants may speak Your word with all confidence'); Isaiah 60:1,2 ('Arise, shine; for your light has come, And the glory of the LORD has risen upon you. For behold, darkness will cover the earth And deep darkness the peoples; But the LORD will rise upon you And His glory will appear upon you'); Revelation 6:15 ('Then the kings of the earth and the great men and the commanders and the rich and the strong and every slave and free man hid themselves in the caves and among the rocks of the mountains'), 15:4 ('Who will not fear, O Lord, and glorify Your name? For You alone are holy; For all the nations will come and worship before you, for your righteous acts have been revealed'); Romans 10:15,18 ('How will they preach unless they are sent? Just as it is written, "How beautiful are the feet of those who bring good news of good things"... But I say, surely they have never heard, have they? Indeed they have; "their voice has gone out into all the earth, and their words to the ends of the world" '); Acts 13:47 ('For so the Lord has commanded us, "I have placed you as a light for the gentiles, that you may bring salvation to the end of the earth." '), 2:21 ('And it shall be that everyone who calls on the name of the Lord will be saved'); 2 Timothy 4:17 ('But the Lord stood with me and strengthened me, so that through me the proclamation might be fully accomplished, and that all the Gentiles might hear; and I was rescued out of the lion's mouth'); 1 John 3:1 ('See how great a love the Father has bestowed on us, that we would be called children of God; and such we are For this reason the world does not know us, because it did not know Him').

[46] 'The nations are now the Lord's; they are His Christ's. For all the Gentiles come before Thee and shall worship Thy name. Now are made manifest Thy glorious law and judgements.' (Revelation 11:15, 15:4)

[47] Including: 'Bonds and affliction abide me there [in Jerusalem]; and ye shall see my face no more' (Acts 20:23,25), 'For I am prepared not only to be bound, but also to die at Jerusalem, for the name of the Lord our saviour Jesus Christ' (Act 21:13), and 'And though he be offered upon the sacrifice of our faith, yet he hath fought a good fight... Henceforth there is laid up for him a crown of righteousness' (2 Timothy 4:7,8).

[48] Sposato recognises the theme of sacrifice but does not make the link to universalism and interprets it as evidence of the influence of contemporary Christological models that see the hero, be it Moses or Paul, as the suffering servant of God whose suffering is brought about by the Jews. Sposato, *The Price of Assimilation*, 92.

Secondly, there is the issue of materials and themes left out by Felix. To anyone familiar with Lutheran understandings of Paul and his life-story, as derived from the book of Acts and his letters, the absence of an explicit reference to the Pauline doctrine of faith alone, or to his abrogation of the Law in that context, or to original sin, or to the Jerusalem Council's decision, after heated debate, to accede to Paul's position that the Gentiles were equally acceptable to God, is puzzling, to say the least.[49] Such omissions were undoubtedly deliberate, as we can see in a complaint that one contributor to the libretto, Schubring, made after Mendelssohn's death.

> That he [Mendelssohn] would not accept my suggestions for the Pauline doctrine of the justification by faith, but, at the appropriate place, substituted merely the general assertion: 'Wir glauben all an einen Gott' [We all believe in one God] was something that did not satisfy my theological conscience, though, perhaps, any extension of the work in this direction would have made it too long.[50]

Put another way, one might ask: to what does Paul convert? Not, as one might have expected from the pen of a convert to Lutheranism, to an understanding of justification by God's grace, and salvation by faith alone in the divine Christ. In fact one is struck by the particular presentation of Jesus.[51] Next to nothing is said of Jesus' messianic role or of his redemptive sacrifice[52] and, certainly, the gloriously powerful cosmic Christ of the Pauline epistles does not emerge from the text. Rather, Jesus is referred to in the context of bringing an end to the Temple and the Law (section 5) and is associated as a martyr with Stephen (section 6). Admittedly, Christ is also seen by Stephen in a vision standing by the side of the Father (section 6), and the unconventional use of women's voices to represent the words of the ascended Christ on the road to Damascus certainly produces an ethereal, otherworldly effect (section 14). But this only reinforces the impression that the *heavenly* Jesus is met only in the subjective visions of men, and there is some evidence that Felix was well aware that such a presentation would be criticised by Protestant theologians.[53] Thus the familiar Lutheran

---

[49] The doctrine of justification by faith alone, that is, the teaching that salvation is brought about through faith in God's grace rather than through works of righteousness, is derived from an interpretation of Ephesians 2:8 ('For by grace you have been saved through faith; and that not of yourselves, it is the gift of God'), an interpretation famously championed by Martin Luther. Accounts of the debate of the early church in Jerusalem are given in Acts 15 and in Galatians 2. Its leader, James, ruled: 'Therefore it is my judgment that we do not trouble those who are turning to God from among the Gentiles, but that we write to them that they abstain from things contaminated by idols and from fornication and from what is strangled and from blood. For Moses from ancient generations has in every city those who preach him, since he is read in the synagogues every Sabbath.' (Acts 15:19–21).

[50] Julius Schubring, 'Reminiscences of Felix Mendelssohn-Bartholdy' reproduced in Todd, ed., *Mendelssohn and His World*, 230. The particular formulation 'We all believe in God' is from a hymn by Martin Luther but Schubring, at least, did not regard it as providing an appropriate emphasis of the doctrine of justification by faith alone.

[51] I am grateful to Canon John Davies, formerly of the University of Southampton, for this observation. Admittedly, this is a somewhat subjective claim since others do identify Christ as a focus to the work. Botstein notes 'the prominence of the figure of Christ in *St. Paul*', referring primarily to the female chorus, and Sposato sees the sacrificial ('suffering servant') motif as Christological in origin. Botstein, 'Songs without Words', 574. Sposato, *The Price of Assimilation*, 92.

[52] Except for three citations of Matthew, the Gospels are completely ignored. Mendelssohn's overwhelming preference is for the Book of Acts (77 citations), in which very little is offered in the way of direct quotations of Jesus.

[53] Felix appears to have been aware that in his revision of the conventions he was sailing close to the wind, theologically speaking, and was courting the condemnation of those who might be suspicious of his religious motives. Schubring recalled that his own suggestion that the voice of Christ be set for four parts ('he [Felix] could not reconcile himself to the notion of producing the effect of a very powerful bass voice'), had a strange effect on Felix: 'After looking at me for a long time, he said: "Yes, and the worthy theologians would cut me up nicely for

reading of Paul that emphasised God's grace as made manifest in the life, death and resurrection of Christ, who redeems the inhabitants of a fallen world through faith alone, is conspicuous by its absence. Jesus appears primarily as a liberator from misguided, outward religion and thereby as a pioneering exemplar for Stephen and Paul.

Felix's portrayal of Paul's story is focused on a God who exists on a plane far beyond the reach of idol or Temple and whose Laws are better observed from the natural world than from the Torah. Furthermore, it champions an understanding of faith that assumes an unchanging ethical core which, from time to time, requires liberation from the religious misunderstandings and theological confusions that human minds (Jewish and Gentile) have accrued over time. The parallels with the views of his father (and grandfather) suggest some obvious sources of influence. But could one not argue that the themes of the libretto could just as likely be explained by more widespread Protestant beliefs? Sposato and Todd both see this particular oratorio as representative of a stage in Felix's life-story when he was concerned to demonstrate his Christian credentials and to achieve his father's goal of assimilation into Prussian society.[54] But contemporary German Lutheran theology, while undoubtedly in intellectual ferment and however varied, can arguably be said to have had offered little in way of encouragement in these directions. On the contrary, one might point to the emergence of Lutheran Confessionalism in the 1830s and 1840s, that is, a movement away from the idea of the Church as the universal Body of Christ and toward a distinctive identity based on traditional Lutheran doctrine and exclusive church worship. Mendelssohn's apparent inclinations towards universalism and even a kind of rationalist, natural religion, as found in *St Paul*, strained against such intellectual currents. The same might be said in relation to the prominent Reformed theologian Friedrich Schleiermacher, a personal friend of Mendelssohn.[55] On the one hand, Schleiermacher recognised that Christianity could claim no monopoly on revelation, believed it impossible to formulate a theology which was valid for all time, and regarded the articles of Christian belief as edifying expressions rather than fixed proofs – all ideas with which Mendelssohn could sympathise. On the other hand, Schleiermacher also gave absolute prominence to Christ in his theology, denied any

---

wishing to deny and supplant Him who arose from the dead."' But he went ahead anyway and had Christ's words set to a four-part female chorus, which did provoke some theological complaints. The composer, 'who was well aware of the circumstance, laughed, but did not say much.' Julius Schubring, 'Reminisences of Felix Mendelssohn-Bartholdy' reproduced in Todd, ed., *Mendelssohn and His World*, 231–232. The other-worldly effect has also been explained as an example of Jewish influence. According to Heinrich Jacob, Felix had applied the commandment 'Thou shalt make thee no graven images' to his music, utilising a device that stressed the great distance between Man and God. Heinrich E. Jacob, *Felix Mendelssohn and His Times*, trans. Richard and Clara Winston (New Jersey: Prentice Hall, 1963), 217.

[54] Todd concludes that 'The completion of the oratorio [*Paulus*] and its successful reception were critical steps towards achieving Abraham's cherished agendum – full assimilation of his family into Prussian society.' Todd, *Mendelssohn: A Life in Music*, 338. Sposato writes that 'Mendelssohn, in this, his first oratorio, tried to assuage real or imagined doubts about his Christian faith by writing a work that conformed to popular expectations, both through its call for the conversion of the nonbelievers and its depiction of the narrow-mindedness of those who refuse to see the light (namely, the Jews). *Paulus* also demonstrates, however, the mental anguish that such a depiction caused Mendelssohn, anguish that led to his eventual reevaluation of this approach... Mendelssohn's tendency to depict the Jews negatively in *Paulus* derived from an overwhelming personal desire to assimilate into German Christian culture.' Sposato, *The Price of Assimilation*, 79, 88.

[55] Felix proclaimed himself 'a follower of Schleiermacher' in 1830 in a letter to his friend Julius Schubring, himself a disciple of the theologian who sought to reconcile Lutheran and Reformed theology; he also cultivated a personal friendship with Schleiermacher. Jeffrey Sposato, *The Price of Assimilation*, 48, 186n39.

meaningful continuity between Judaism and Christianity (dismissing Judaism as almost entirely without value), and emphasised religious feeling over and against what he saw as the simplistic rationalism of natural theologians and deists – ideas which seem at odds with the reading of the theology underlying the libretto given here.[56]

Finally, it is useful to consider Felix's treatment of the apostle in the context of Jewish approaches to Paul more generally. However counter-intuitive it may seem, Mendelssohn's treatment of Paul is entirely inline with a number of Jewish commentaries on Paul and, in particular, with several artistic Jewish renderings of the apostle in the modern period, including those of a painter, a playwright, and two novelists.[57] Their treatments, like Mendelssohn's, tended to reflect highly idiosyncratic views of the two religions, and the underlying themes of the oratorio resonate powerfully in their works. In a context where the centuries-old rules no longer seem to apply, there was a shared need to map out the relationship between Jews and Gentiles. For those who inhabited the religious and cultural borderlands, there was a common struggle to achieve a coherent, satisfactory resolution, and a feeling that Paul was a figure close to the heart of the issue. But above all, the key concern was whether or not there existed a common religious essence between Judaism and Christianity. It is worth noting that the majority agreed that there was, despite maintaining that Paul was responsible for the 'parting of the ways'. Its precise nature was described variously in their treatments of the apostle in terms of an underlying rationality, or prophetic inspiration, or complementary manifestations of the spirit of God, or a universal brotherhood of faith. It may be correct to limit what Sposato has described as Mendelssohn's 'attempt to reconcile his Christian faith and his Jewish heritage' to the later oratorio *Elijah*,[58] but it seems

---

[56] Schleiermacher wrote that 'Christianity... is essentially distinguished from other such faiths by the fact that in it everything is related to the redemption accomplished by Jesus of Nazareth... Christianity cannot in any wise be regarded as a remodelling or a renewal and continuation of Judaism... Neither can it be said that purer original Judaism carried within itself the germ of Christianity... [Except for prophecy] almost everything else in the Old Testament is, for our Christian usage, but the husk or wrapping of its prophecy, and that whatever is most definitely Jewish has least value'. Friedrich Schleiermacher, *The Christian Faith*, trans. by H.R. Mackintosh and J.S. Stewart (Edinburgh: T&T Clark, 1999), 52, 61, 62. German original: *Der christliche Glaube* (Berlin: 1821–22). For Sposato, Schleiermacher's anti-Judaic sentiments are indicative of Mendelssohn's own position. Sposato, *The Price of Assimilation*, 93–94. Schleiermacher's attitude towards natural religion and the 'empiricism' of deism was highly critical: 'The essence of natural religion actually consists wholly in the negation of everything positive and characteristic in religion and in the most violent polemic against it.' Friedrich Schleiermacher, *On Religion*, trans. Richard Crouter (Cambridge: Cambridge University Press, 1988), 192, 207. German original: *Reden über die Religion* (Berlin: 1799). This attitude stems from his central project, as described by one commentator: 'The way in which God is apprehended in the immediacy of feeling of utter dependence... leads [Schleiermacher] to a conception of the relation of God and the world which does not fit into the common classifications of deism, theism, pantheism... He was plainly seeking a view beyond naturalism and supernaturalism. Deism was obviously abhorrent, for it posits an externality of God to the world and the self that is utterly at odds with the feeling of utter dependence, and makes God only "a being."' Claude Welsch, *Protestant Thought in the Nineteenth Century: 1799–1870* (New Haven: Yale University Press, 1972), I:79.

[57] Ludwig Meidner, 'Pauluspredigt' (Paul's Sermon, 1919), watercolour, 68x49cm. Buller Collection, Duisberg. Franz Werfel, *Paulus unter den Juden* (Berlin: Zsolnay, 1926). Sholem Asch, *The Apostle*, trans. by Maurice Samuel (London: Macdonald, 1949). Samuel Sandmel, *The Apostle Paul: A Novel* (unpublished, undated), 472pp, in Samuel Sandmel Papers, Manuscript Collection No. 101, Series C/1/17.7 and 18.1 at the American Jewish Archives, Cincinnati, U.S.A.

[58] Sposato suggests that a changing attitude towards Jews is apparent from the time of Felix's revival of the St. Matthew Passion in 1829, through the libretto drafted for A.B. Marx's *Mose* in 1833 and the oratorios of *St. Paul* (1836), *Elijah* (1846), and *Christ* (1847). The new attitude revealed in the last two works was 'one no longer fuelled by a need to demonize the Jews in order to prove the sincerity of his Christian faith.' Sposato, *The Price of Assimilation*, 178–179.

reasonable to trace this activity back to his earlier study of *St Paul*, too. If that is indeed the case, then it is worth pointing out that this struggle is by no means unique to this Protestant composer of Jewish heritage – it is arguably a characteristic concern of a number of Jewish engagements with the Apostle to the Gentiles in the modern period.

BIBLIOGRAPHY

Botstein, Leon, 'Songs without Words: Thoughts on Music, Theology, and the Role of the Jewish Question in the Work of Felix Mendelssohn', *The Musical Quarterly* 77:4 (Winter 1993).

Botstein Leon, 'The Aesthetics of Assimilation and Affirmation: Reconstructing the Career of Felix Mendelssohn' in R. Larry Todd, ed., *Mendelssohn and His World* (Princeton: Princeton University Press, 1991).

Botstein, Leon, 'Mendelssohn and the Jews', *The Musical Quarterly* 82:1 (Spring 1998).

Cohen, Shaye J.D., *The Beginnings of Jewishness: Boundaries, Varieties, Uncertainties* (Berkley: University of California Press, 1999).

Devrient, Eduard, *Meine Erinnerungen an Felix Mendelssohn* (Leipzig: J.J. Weber, 1872).

Hensel, Sebastian, *The Mendelssohn Family*, trans. Carl Klingemann, second edition (New York: Harper, 1882).

Jacob, Heinrich E., *Felix Mendelssohn and His Times*, trans. Richard and Clara Winston (New Jersey: Prentice Hall, 1963).

Krausz, Michael, 'On Being Jewish' in David Theo Goldberg and Michael Krausz, eds., *Jewish Identity* (Philadelphia: Temple University Press, 1993).

Langton, Daniel R., *The Apostle Paul in the Jewish Imagination* (Cambridge: Cambridge University Press, 2010).

Mendelssohn-Bartholdy, Felix, *Paulus* (Bonn: N. Simrock, 1836).

Mendelssohn, Felix, *St. Paul* (Birmingham: 1837).

Mendelssohn, Moses, *Phaedon or the Death of Socrates* (London: J. Cooper, 1789).

Mendelssohn, Moses, *Jerusalem or On Religious Power and Judaism*, trans. Allan Arkush (New England: Brandeis, 1983).

Schneider, M., *Mendelssohn oder Bartholdy?* (Basel: Internationale Felix-Mendelssohn-Gesellschaft, 1962).

Sposato, Jeffrey S., 'Creative Writing: The [Self-] Identification of Mendelssohn as a Jew', *The Musical Quarterly* 82:1 (Spring 1998).

Sposato, Jeffrey S., 'Mendelssohn, 'Paulus', and the Jews: A Response to Leon Botstein and Michael Steinberg', *The Musical Quarterly* 83:2 (Summer 1999).

Sposato, Jeffrey, *The Price of Assimilation: Felix Mendelssohn and the Nineteenth-Century Anti-Semitic Tradition* (Oxford: Oxford University Press, 2006).

Steinberg, Michael P., 'Mendelssohn's Music and German-Jewish Culture: An Intervention', *The Musical Quarterly* 83:1 (Spring 1999).

Todd, R. Larry, *Mendelssohn: A Life in Music* (Oxford: Oxford University Press, 2003).

Wagner, Richard, *Judaism in Music and other Writings*, trans. W. Ashton Ellis (London: University of Nebraska Press, 1995).

Werner, Eric, *A New Image of the Composer and his Age*, trans. Dika Newlin (New York: Collier-Macmillan, 1963).

THE ORDINARINESS OF BEING JEWISH: JEWISH 'NORMALITY' IN MANCHESTER, 1830–1880

Bill Williams*

Between anti-Semitic and Whig presentations of the history of Anglo-Jewry lies the occasionally uncomfortable reality of Jewish normality. Despite the best efforts of the Anglo-Jewish elites, British Jews did not always behave as they were expected to do, and the city of Manchester in the Victorian period provides an excellent window onto the world of everyday Jewish diaspora life. It was a bustling city characterized by massive immigrant settlement, which juxtaposed popular anti-alien sentiment and the self-congratulatory platitudes of liberal Mancunians. Looking beyond the defensive posturing of local Jewish community leaders such as Nathan Laski, the historian is led to the sordid reality of bankruptcy, domestic violence, theft, perjury, con-artistry, assault, gambling, and prostitution. The argument presented here is that the danger of constructing Jewish life in terms of a rose-tinted collective mythology – or in terms of an anti-Semitic obsession with Jewish difference – can be tempered by the notion of 'Jewish ordinariness'.

Conceptions of Jewish 'normality' are significant not only for the study of Anglo-Jewry, but also for understanding the perspectives of the social historians of Anglo-Jewry. The kinds of evidence which any social historian uses quickly reveal major differences in perception of the 19th century Anglo-Jewish experience. One perspective is that of the anti-Semite, whose narrative flows through deep-seated and all-too-familiar stereotypes. Although these hostile images are highly flexible, occasionally subtle and sometimes difficult to detect, historians are now sufficiently well-equipped with knowledge of how anti-Semitism might arise and the forms it might take to unravel the reality from the distortions. Another perspective has been described as a 'Whig' interpretation of Jewish history: Jewish history, that is, as a narrative of 'progress' under the auspices of a largely benevolent communal leadership in an essentially liberal society. Currently this perspective is being slowly, but radically, unpicked by a new generation of historians which includes, amongst many others, David Cesarani, Tony Kushner and David Feldman, all of whom have rejected a Whig orthodoxy usually traced to Cecil Roth.

This essay touches on what may be seen as another significant disjunction in Anglo-Jewish history: that between what is often presented as the 'normality' of 19th century Jewish communal life, and what might be described as its actuality, even as its 'ordinariness'. It is another sharp clash of images, here between, on the one hand, images projected by Jewish communal leaders, the Jewish press, and liberal Judaeophiles, of what the 19th century community was like, or rather how they wished it to be seen (or, for that matter, what they thought it *ought* to be like), and the realities of Manchester's late Victorian Jewry. The

* Hon. Research Fellow, Centre for Jewish Studies, University of Manchester. Email: billwilliams31@ btinternet.com This paper was not originally given at the BAJS conference in 2008, but its theme and the important contribution that it makes to the discussion on normativity in Judaism justify its inclusion here.

suggestion here is that the contrasting images may be traced to a diasporic experience in which the Jewish community had somehow to adjust to life in a non-Jewish setting. While the experience itself was common to all Jewish communities, the precise narratives to which it gave rise differ in detail from country to country and town to town.

In this chapter, the place and period of focus is late 19th century Manchester Jewry, particularly the community of the 1870s and 1880s, a period during which Jewish immigration from Eastern Europe was gathering pace and in which Manchester Jewry was subject to verbal attack from those who took objection to the size and what they saw as the nature of new immigrant settlement. It was a time, it might be argued, when the Jewish community was thrown on the defensive and when it seemed particularly important to the Jewish leadership to present images of communal life which somehow countered those of the anti-alien and the anti-Semite. It was a time, too, when liberal Christians felt the need to come out and be counted. Such strategies, however, both began earlier and continued long after the most intense phase of anti-alienism ended.

The Manchester Narrative

The public discourse which accompanied the quest for Jewish emancipation between 1830 and 1858 persuaded the leaders of the Jewish community in Manchester (as elsewhere) that it had somehow to 'prove' its entitlement to political equality. Communal leaders were made to feel that they had to show that Manchester Jews were (or were likely to become) sufficiently educated, anglicised, law-abiding, patriotic and civic minded to merit their elevation into full citizenship of the British state. This was also the hope of those who actually led the quest for emancipation. In Manchester these were cotton merchants of Dutch and German origin and a few successful retail traders: people, that is, who by 1830 had already achieved economic and social standing. It was in the interests of such leaders, both as a class and as Jews, to so 'improve' the community that its political future (and their social standing) would be assured. The Jewish middle-classes were also those most likely to achieve personal benefits from emancipation, in the shape of municipal or national office, as indeed they did.

In the case of a local non-Jewish liberal elite in Manchester, support for Jewish emancipation was both an expression and a proof of the liberalism of their New Athens. Since the 1820s their chief mouthpiece, the *Manchester Guardian*, had contrasted the anti-Semitism of other countries with the welcome accorded to Jews by Manchester. Typically such gestures were accompanied by praise of 'those Jews who live amongst us' (chiefly, at this point, German and Dutch merchants and shopkeepers). They were law-abiding, sober, respectable, civic-minded and benevolent. They had undergone, it was left unsaid, the transforming chemistry of liberalism.

The inner 'improvement' of the Jewish community in preparation for its political freedom began in 1838 with the creation of a Manchester Hebrew Association whose self-appointed tasks were to organise an elementary education for Jewish children from poorer families (their own were educated by home tutors or in private academies) and to arrange for sermons in English to be delivered in the community's only synagogue, then a tiny, unadorned building in Halliwell Street near the centre of Manchester. Within two or three years, both these tasks had been accomplished. After toying with the idea of sending Jewish children to such non-Jewish schools as the Lyceums of Manchester and Salford, the Association opted for a Jewish elementary school, the Manchester Jews School, which opened in rented accommodation on Cheetham Hill Road, the heart of Manchester's Jewish Quarter, in 1840. A religious minister capable to delivering sermons in English was recruited from the older, and then larger, Jewish community in neighbouring Liverpool.[1]

What mattered most to the Association's committee, led by the affluent and probably Jamaican-born cotton manufacturer, Philip Lucas, was not so much the reality of communal life as its image: how it was seen by others. Sometimes this was made explicit. Jacob Franklin, son of a Manchester optician (and later to become editor of Anglo-Jewry's first newspaper, *The Voice of Jacob*) spoke of raising 'the character of our nation in the estimation of others'.[2] The changes thought necessary by the Association clearly promoted the image of a community seeking respectability through anglicisation. The legacy of the emancipation 'struggle' was the continuing emphasis of its leaders not on how the community was, but how it looked. There were few Christian outsiders, at least at this stage in communal history, who had the will or the opportunity to assess the community from within.

It also tickled the humanitarian ego of the native middle-classes to go along with an image which appeared to confirm their liberality and its consequences. In their eyes Jews were 'well-ordered and educated', 'peaceable and law abiding', 'a most wealthy and respectable section of the Manchester world', 'liberal in principle and purse', 'eminently loyal and useful citizens', 'high in reputation for wealth and charity', a 'straightforward and remarkably sober class or people'. For the liberal middle-classes the enemy within was not the Jew, who, in their eyes, had clearly come to adopt middle-class values, but the (supposedly) 'riotous' and drunken Irishman.[3]

Jewish communal leaders, with power both within the community and outside it, also served as mediators, particularly in the setting up of 'ritual occasions', when middle-class Jews met up formally with middle-class Mancunians and civic dignitaries, and when each was expected to lavish praise on the other. The events might be anything from an annual general meeting of a communal charity to the consecration of new synagogues (on one occasion it was to confer a 'civic blessing' on a new *mikvah*). Such otherwise empty occasions of mutual praise served to confirm the community's integration into the city, and the city's reciprocal tolerance. On occasion mediation assumed a personal character, as when, in the 1880s, Henry Samson, a Reform Jew, was president of the Jewish Board of Guardians, while his business partner in the export trade, Henry Leppoc, a Jewish convert to Unitarian Christianity, served as chairman of the Manchester Poor Law Guardians. More frequently it represented the close bonds of class, apparently strong enough to overcome differences in religion and heritage.

The generation of leaders typified by Lucas, who in 1851 became Manchester's first Jewish city councillor and who exercised communal power during the 1870s and 80s, was

---

[1] Bill Williams, *The Making of Manchester Jewry 1740–1875* (Manchester: Manchester University Press, 1976), 88–103.

[2] Manchester Hebrew Association, 'First Annual Report' (1839), 5 in 'Annual Reports for Manchester Hebrew Association, 1839-1867', held by the Manchester Room at the Central Reference Library, Manchester, 372.942, M28.

[3] Bill Williams, 'The Anti-Semitism of Tolerance: Middle-Class Manchester and the Jews 1870–1900' in A.J. Kidd and K.W. Roberts, eds., *City, Class and Culture: Studies of cultural production and social policy in Victorian Manchester* (Manchester: Manchester University Press,1985), 74–76.

made up largely of a minor plutocracy of merchants and industrialists engaged in the manufacture or export of cotton goods, and highly successful retailers like Benjamin Hyam, Manchester's first manufacturer of ready-made clothes: a miniature, but localised version of the London 'Cousinhood'.[4] It was they who served as the patrons and managers of such communal educational, social and welfare organisations as the Manchester Jews School, the Manchester Jewish Board of Guardians, founded in 1867 on the model of a similar organisation created earlier in London, and the Jewish Working Men's Club, founded in the early 1880s, also after a London blueprint. It was they who felt called upon, although as much to preserve their own hard-won status as to protect the community, to respond to the anti-alienism of sections of the Manchester press. It was they who shaped the flow of 'official' communal news to the non-Jewish press and to the Jewish press in London. It was they who felt the need to ally themselves with their liberal Christian peers, who, in turn, found in the situation another opportunity to advertise their liberality.

The contrast between an idealised version of communal life and a more complex normality is to be found in the contrast between, on the one hand, the official reports of Jewish institutions, the official pronouncements of the London Jewish press (Manchester had no Jewish newspaper of its own until the 1930s) and the pronouncements of Manchester's liberal elite, amply reported by the *Manchester Guardian*, and, on the other, the spontaneous, unmediated reports of events involving Jews in the more parochial and less liberal sectors of the local press, typified by the weekly *Manchester City News*.

Images and Realities, 1870s and 80s

Official reports from the Jews School, the Jewish Board of Guardians and the Jewish Working Men's Club (JWMC) intended for the local press went out of their way to stress the charitable intentions of Jewish leaders, the merits and potential for citizenship of the Eastern European immigrants then under attack as 'undesireable aliens', and the ways in which the JWMC was introducing immigrants to English social etiquette, English forms of leisure, English patriotism and the English language. It was claimed that the work of the Jewish Board of Guardians and the Jews School was 'superior' to that of the English Poor Law because it 'had introduced into it the feelings of charity and religion [and] had endeavoured to uphold the cause of education and charity.' It had offered the Jewish poor 'those manifestations of sympathy to which they were accustomed'; unlike the Poor Law, the Jewish Board did not 'pauperise' its applicants, but had simply 'given as a charity for which they have a right to ask.'[5]

Poorer Jewish immigrants also supposedly differed from the applicants to the Poor Law. They were not by nature 'paupers', but the victims of temporary misfortune. They looked to the Board only for initial help towards economic independence. Their 'foreignness' was also temporary, a 'Ghetto bend' which philanthropy would iron out. If not themselves always as open to immediate change as they might be, the children of immigrants, it was said, would soon adjust to English standards of behaviour and the obligations of English citizenship.

---

[4] Williams, *The Making of Manchester Jewry*, Chapter 4; 'The Plutocracy'.
[5] AGM of the Manchester Jewish Board of Guardians, as reported in the *Manchester City News* (hereafter *MCN*), 21 June 1879.

Meantime they were hard-working, religiously devout, imbued with exceptional loyalty to their families, and as anxious themselves to escape pauperism and become economically independent as Manchester was to keep them off the rates.

The London Jewish press reserved a brief column for Manchester news, which was made up of the formal activities of Jewish charities, the foundation (and committeemen) of new synagogues and societies, Jewish achievements (scholarships, medals, presidencies, elections to the city council), and the kind of ritual occasions intended to confirm Jewish-Christian harmony. Obituaries of the Jewish great and good were accompanied by notes of the progress of the aspiring in communal life and/or English politics.

All this was underwritten by liberal Mancunians, whose praise for the Jews reached what might be seen an extreme of liberal narcissism, in part to distance themselves from equally extreme Czarist persecution of Russian Jewry. In 1882, at a public meeting to decry Russian anti-Semitism, John Slagg, a Manchester Liberal MP, summarised his view of Jewish emancipation:

> In every country where they were allowed full rights and privileges of citizenship they conformed to the laws of that country: they blended with its institutions and they constituted an element in their societies of the finest and most useful description… [W]e had no better Englishmen in England than the Jews. [In Manchester] the Jewish community… constituted one of our greatest ornaments. They were, whether considered socially in their aspect as merchants or in any other relationship of citizenship, an element of the community of which the people of Manchester might be and were justly very proud.[6]

This was the Jewish community as its leaders wished it to be seen: a respectable, anglicised, philanthropic, and loyal middle-class, paving the way to integration, civic virtue and patriotism for newcomers anxious only to find their feet and contribute to the well-being and economy of the city.

Jewish Ordinariness

It is not so much a matter of such an image being entirely false as being very far from complete, as air-brushing out everything which might suggest an alternative. No doubt Slagg was right in his account of Jewish merchants. What is absent is the other two-thirds of a community then numbering around 7,000, particularly, the Yiddish-speaking Eastern European immigrants, who had been arriving since the mid-1840s,[7] living in 1882 in overcrowded slums like Red Bank and Strangeways (about to attract the attention of the xenophobe and the anti-Semite), working long hours for low pay in cramped and insanitary clothing and furniture workshops and living a religious life in makeshift *chevroth* separate not only from the city but from their richer co-religionists.

But the divorce of image from reality was more than demographic. In the pages of the *Manchester City News*, edited, it is true, by the nativist, John Nodal, associated with a group of less than mediocre anecdotalists, antiquarians and aspiring writers and artists, there emerges a community like any other: with elements and individuals mired (as in any other) in extreme

---

[6] *Manchester Guardian*, 4 February 1882.
[7] Williams, *The Making of Manchester Jewry*, Chapter 11: 'The Immigrant Poor'.

poverty, petty criminality, social disorder, violence, murder, fraud, prostitution, sexual misdemeanour, and inter-filial betrayal.

Between 1875 and 1882 (the year of Slagg's speech), interspersed with news of Jewish office-holders at the Royal Manchester Institution, the spectacular donations to charity of a Jewish optician, William Aronsberg, the presentation of an oil painting to Henry Julius Leppoc for his work on the Manchester Board of Guardians,[8] Jewish shareholders in the Manchester Aquarium,[9] commissions awarded to Jewish members of Manchester Volunteer Regiments, Jewish invitees to the Lord Mayor's Juvenile Ball,[10] Jews present at the Lord Mayor's 'grand soiree',[11] Jewish language teachers and chess-players at the Manchester Athenaeum,[12] and an admiring article on 'Jews in the Yarn Trade',[13] are *City News* reports of the following:

An itinerant Jewish shoemaker housed in a lodging house for foreigners situated in Crown Square, the most squalid sector of Manchester's worst slum, Angel Meadow, absconding to Liverpool with the takings of a fellow-lodger, also Jewish;[14]

Two Jewish pawnbrokers fined for 'detaining' the watches pledged by clients, others for using illegal weights;[15]

The palatial mansion of a bankrupted Jewish merchant sold, with all its contents, by public auction;[16]

Five Jewish lodging-house keepers with property in Red Bank fined for overcrowding on information supplied by the Superintendant of the Manchester Nuisance Department;[17]

Esther, Louis and Moses Feinberg and Moses Frankel, all of Strangeways (one focus of Eastern European Jewish settlement), as part of a gang which stole £1,000's worth of silk from a Manchester warehouse; the police caught up with them in London. The *City News* carried regular reports of their trial and conviction in the City Police Court and the Manchester Quarter Sessions (and imprisonment) under the heading 'The Great Silk Robberies';[18]

Harris Kimeroski deserting his wife and family (who are thus confined in the Manchester Workhouse) and turning up in a 'low lodging house' in Liverpool, where, until the police catch up with him, he is preparing to cross the Atlantic, 'with a young woman';[19]

Louis Kaufman, a tobacconist, appearing in the City Police Court for defrauding a firm of stockbrokers by false representation. One of his witnesses, also Jewish, is charged with perjury. Although both are acquitted (to 'cheering and clapping of hands' from Kaufman's friends in court) the Stipendiary magistrate comments: 'Technically, I don't think you can prove a case... I won't say anything about what it is morally';[20]

---

[8] *MCN*, 12 May 1877.
[9] *MCN*, 7 July 1877.
[10] *MCN*, 10 January 1880.
[11] *MCN*, 23 January 1875
[12] *MCN*, 3 and 10 February 1877.
[13] *MCN*, 31 January 1880.
[14] *MCN*, 2 January 1875.
[15] *MCN*, 16 January 1875; 17 January 1880.
[16] *MCN*, 20 March 1875.
[17] *MCN*, 12 June 1875.
[18] *MCN*, 19, 26 June; 10 July 1875.
[19] *MCN*, 27 November 1875.
[20] *MCN*, 28 October; 18 November 1875.

A Jewish quack doctor, Isaac J. Lewis, fined for describing himself as an MD and selling worthless cures;[21]

The wife of a Jewish export merchant imprisoned for 12 months for shop-lifting two shawls, three yards of velvet, two neck furs, 25 pairs of gloves, 16 stockings, one muffler, three yards of belting, 64 yards of ribbons, 54 yards of ribbon velvet, one flower and one feather;[22]

Conflict between Jewish merchants taken to the Civil Court, which suggest that the Jewish plutocracy was nothing like as coherent as its public face;[23]

A Jewish money-lender fined for damage to property in an attempt to seize the furniture of one of his clients, who is stabbed in the process by one of a gang of thirty men;[24]

Trapowski, a jeweller in Strangeways, taken to court by the Chorlton Board of Guardians and ordered to pay for the maintenance of a wife, also Jewish, whom he had deserted. In court he stated that 'he was willing to pay for her in the [Union] Workhouse' (which lacked facilities for kosher meals);[25]

Mary Blundell, a prostitute, occupying one of the 'disorderly' houses in Chorlton-on-Medlock, let furnished and cheaply by a Jewish merchant, Maurice Youngerman, who said 'he could find her another... if there was any bother';[26]

An illegal still found in the house rented by a Jewish family in Red Bank, with bottles of wine in the gutters;[27]

Michael Chefnoski, a Jewish tailor residing in Beswick's Row, Angel Meadow, gaoled for one month for neglecting his wife and child. He is described as 'a great gambler' who abused his wife, once threatening to strike her with a [tailor's] sleeve board.[28]

Much of this was trivia. Some of it was perhaps given undue publicity because of the Jewish identity (often noted) of the perpetrator, but what it offers is part of a more accurate view of Jewish normality. So do significant aspects (omitted in their official reports) of Jewish educational and philanthropic bodies, particularly the intensity of their hostility to Yiddish and to aspects of immigrant religiosity regarded as 'un-English'. Most recipients of charity from the Jewish Board of Guardians were Orthodox; many of the managers Reform. To keep the immigrants on the move, financial support could be offered only once during an immigrant's first six months of residence in Manchester. Support of any kind was refused to parents who would not send their children to the (anglicising) Jews School or who belonged to 'clandestine societies' (that is, *chevroth*). Immigrant children arriving at the Jews School with Yiddish first names had them forcibly changed to names that were recognisably English (so Tauba became Matilda).

The idea that the Jewish Board was more 'sympathetic' to applicants than public charities, although true in some of the details of its mechanisms, needs to be read with the reservation that the Jewish Boards in London and Manchester were modelled on the Boards of

---

[21] *MCN*, 28 October 1876,
[22] *MCN*, 16 December 1876; 13 January 1877.
[23] *MCN*, 23 January 1878.
[24] *MCN*, 16 November 1878; 26 January 1879.
[25] *MCN*, 23 August 1879.
[26] *MCN*, 13 September 1879.
[27] *MCN*, 8 March 1884.
[28] *MCN*, 3 April 1880.

Guardians of the English Poor Law Unions, with their typical rejection of the 'undeserving poor'. Jewish wives temporarily deserted by husbands who had gone ahead to the United States were routinely incarcerated in Union Workhouses.

The Continuity of Image-making

During the 1880s and 90s the old mercantile elite was gradually displaced by a new communal leadership made up of successful entrepreneurs of Eastern European (and chiefly Russian) origin. These were men who, after starting life on the unremunerative shop-floors of small clothing and furniture workshops, or as clerks in the warehouses of export merchants, had, by their skill and enterprise, risen to become entrepreneurs, at first on a small scale, and, in some cases, subsequently as the owners of factories each employing 1,000 works or more. Most were manufacturers of what had been the staple product of earlier workshops: clothing and furniture, footwear, cloth caps, cigarettes and waterproof garments. A few branched into cotton after apprenticeships typically with their merchant co-religionists of German, Dutch or Sephardi origin.

One of these latter was Nathan Laski, born in Russian Poland, and brought to England in the 1860s as a child by his parents, first to Middleborough, then to Manchester. His father, who in Manchester became a 'jewellery traveller', sent his son to the Manchester Jews School and, when he left, found him a clerical apprenticeship with a German firm of export traders. Laski rose quickly to become first a partner in the firm and then, with one of his brothers, an export merchant on his own account. A man of striking appearance, rich oratorical powers and dictatorial inclinations, with a particular gift for fund-raising and mediation, he moved fairly rapidly up the ladder of communal institutions to become, by 1891 the youngest ever president of the Manchester Great Synagogue, by 1910 president of the Jewish Board of Guardians, the Manchester Shechita Board and the Manchester Victoria Jewish Hospital, and in 1924 president of the Manchester and Salford Jewish Representative Council, a position he held with only a brief interruption, until his death (in a motor accident) in 1942.

From his predecessors Laski inherited what had become the major strategy designed to protect the security and inner life of the community, that is, the manufacture and promotion of an imagery deemed to correspond with what Christian Manchester had by then learned to accept: respectable, stable, law-abiding, civic-minded and eminently English. With powerful contacts within the Christian city, as a merchant, magistrate and a Liberal (he became chairman of the Liberal Association of North Manchester, in which capacity, he helped secure the 1905 victory of Winston Churchill, then a Liberal, in the North-West Manchester constituency), he was in the ideal position for mediation. This he did with deferential aplomb. At the time of Queen Victoria's death he had the whole of the (very large) Great Synagogue draped in black. He attended Christian services and invited his Christian friends to attend synagogue on special occasions. He was openly critical of those communal institutions he judged to be un-English: the Manchester *Yeshivah*, for example, which conducted its teaching in Yiddish and which avoided secular learning.

Laski was a master-craftsman in the construction and sustaining of images of Jewish respect for the law, orderly conduct and patriotism. At his mansion in Smedley Lane, a plusher sector of Cheetham Hill, he chaired a private 'court' which dealt with minor offences and communal disputes before they could reach open court. It is said that by the time of his death he had adjudicated in hundreds of such cases. When refugees began to seek entry to Britain from Germany after 1933, although he associated himself with the Central British Fund, he did all he could to keep them away from Manchester, where they might have suggested a renewal of the 'alien invasion', of which his own family had been part, and which had then attracted fierce anti-Jewish feeling in the city. He warned Jewish anti-Fascists to desist from militant confrontation with Mosley's Blackshirts, as he had warned others to avoid causing any kind of disorder on the Manchester streets. Before 1938, when *Kristallnacht* and the British response to it finally persuaded him to promote Manchester committees for their reception, he took no public action to ease the settlement of refugees in Manchester. Nor did he publicise in Manchester the terrors faced by German Jews, though he knew of them well enough, for fear of alienating a government which had settled for appeasement. It might be said that he took image-making to its very highest levels.

There is a real danger of the history and heritage of the Jewish community being constructed out of images which have melded into a collective mythology. By detaching the Jewish experience from the more rounded experiences of others, this might achieve a result far from that intended: delivering to the anti-Semite just that separate and distinct target they most crave. It might, by sharply differentiating the experience of Jews from that of other and later immigrants, persuade Jews that in some way their experience was qualitatively different from that of other newcomers to British society, and therefore irrelevant to their understanding. It might persuade Jews, historians and others that the images somehow constitute Jewish normality.

BIBLIOGRAPHY

Williams, Bill, *The Making of Manchester Jewry 1740–1875* (Manchester: Manchester University Press, 1976).

Williams, Bill, 'The Anti-Semitism of Tolerance: Middle-Class Manchester and the Jews 1870–1900' in A.J. Kidd and K.W. Roberts, eds., *City, Class and Culture: Studies of cultural production and social policy in Victorian Manchester* (Manchester: Manchester University Press, 1985).

Manchester City News (1875–1884).

Manchester Guardian (1882).

Annual reports for Manchester Hebrew Association, 1839–1867. Manchester Room at the Central Reference Library, Manchester, 372.942, M28.

'NORMATIVE JUDAISM' IN THE CRISIS OF WAR: SERMONS BY ABRAHAM COHEN AND ISRAEL MATTUCK

Marc Saperstein*

This study explores the conception of 'normative Judaism' in early 20th-century Britain through an analysis of unpublished sermons delivered during the First World War by an Orthodox and a Liberal preacher near the beginning of what would be illustrious careers. Common themes are exemplified in powerfully impressive passages from these sermons: the shock at the outbreak of a European-wide conflict and its challenge to widespread assumptions about civilization and progress; a strong sense that the apparent causes could not justify such bloodshed in tension with the desire to find some idealistic rationale for the war; ambivalence about siding with Czarist Russia against Germany and Austria, each with a far better record regarding their Jewish populations; the crucial importance for British Jews to demonstrate loyalty to their country; theological anguish and the question of why God permits the horrors to continue; the need to articulate an appropriate role for prayer (especially at national Intercession Services) despite the awareness that Jews and Christians in enemy nations were also praying for victory in the sincere belief that theirs was the cause of justice; a rejection of naïve optimism about the goals to be achieved as a result of the conflict. On each of these points, the position taken by the two preachers was almost interchangeable, suggesting that the concept of an over-arching Anglo-Judaism during this period is not without basis. Further comparison with contemporary war-time French and German Jewish preaching – in which the patriotic dimension and negative discourse about the enemy appears to be far more pronounced than in the British examples – will be illuminating.

In this essay, I propose to explore one small aspect of the concept of 'normativity' in Judaism by reviewing the unpublished sermons of two preachers from very different positions on the spectrum of Anglo-Jewry delivered during World War I.

First is the Orthodox Rev Abraham Cohen (1887–1957) of Birmingham. Educated at Emmanuel College, Cambridge, he continued Jewish studies in Manchester and eventually earned a Ph.D. from the University of London.[1] In 1913 he came to the Birmingham Hebrew Congregation of Singer's Hill, where he would serve for some 36 years, becoming highly esteemed in the community and widely known beyond it for his publications on classical Jewish texts. His Sieff Lectures on Preaching at Jews' College were published as a wonderful handbook of guidance in preparing and delivering a sermon.[2]

---

* Professor of Jewish History and Homiletics at Leo Baeck College, London. Email: marc.saperstein@lbc.ac.uk

[1] Following the custom of British Jewry, Cohen did not use the title Rabbi; at first it was 'Rev', then 'Rev Dr'.

[2] Rev A. Cohen, *Jewish Homiletics* (London: ML Cailingold, 1937); the actual texts of his sermons reveal how he implemented these guidelines over three and a half decades. In addition to such popular scholarly works as *Everyman's Talmud* (London: JM Dent, 1932) and *The Soncino Chumash* (Hindhead: Soncino, 1947), Cohen's wide reading in what he calls 'the by-paths of English literature' is revealed in an illuminating anthology of English travel literature describing actual Jewish communities throughout the world: *An Anglo-Jewish Scrapbook, 1600–1940: The Jew Through English Eyes* (London: M. L. Cailingold, 1943). He also served as president of the Board of Deputies from 1949–1955, the only religious leader to have held this position: Raphael Langham, *250 Years of Convention and Contention* (London: Vallentine Mithecll, 2010), 180.

Israel Mattuck (1883–1954) was born in Lithuania and educated in America at Harvard (where he studied Semitics with Professor George Foot Moore) and the Hebrew Union College, Cincinnati. When Claude G. Montefiore consulted leaders of American Reform Judaism for advice on finding an appropriate rabbi for the Jewish Religious Union, Mattuck was recommended. He first preached for the Union in June 1911 and was swiftly invited to become Minister by the Council. Mattuck was inducted to his position by Montefiore in January 1912, and soon became a major figure in the Jewish Religious Union, attracting large numbers of people to the London synagogue.[3]

Thus both men came to their positions in a significant Jewish community shortly before the war began, Cohen in 1913, Mattuck in 1912; they both remained actively involved through the Second World War. Both of these men were known as powerful, eloquent preachers, and the texts of their sermons confirm that reputation. The unpublished texts of these sermons[4] are a rich source documenting the perceptions and responses by Jewish religious leaders to events universally recognized as being of staggering historical importance. They also provide a test case for measuring the extent of diversity within Anglo-Jewry during this critical period. Because the material is inaccessible in print, I will illustrate with extensive quotation from the manuscripts.

Cohen preached about the war during the first two Shabbat services following England's formal entrance as a combatant, August 8 and 15. As Mattuck apparently did not preach in the month of August, one natural comparison would be with a series of Shabbat sermons from August 1914 by the German Liberal Rabbi, Julius Jelski[5] – but that would be a different paper. (In general, what is absent from these sermons by Cohen is the patriotic fervour so powerful in sermons by contemporary French, German and Austrian rabbis.)[6] What were the dominant themes in Cohen's sermons from the very first weeks?

First, the shock that a war of apparently unprecedented dimensions could have broken out in 20th-century Europe. Almost 100 years had passed since the entire continent had been convulsed in this way (the Franco-Prussian War presented a similar shock, but was limited to two major powers). During that century, many had come to believe that the progress of civilisation toward greater enlightenment, toward the peaceful resolution of disputes, was irreversible. The new war presented a shattering challenge to these assumptions. On 8 August 1914, Shabbat *Naḥamu*, which Cohen says brings no comfort this year, he asserts that the outbreak of war was especially troubling for Jews:

---

[3] On Mattuck, see Lawrence Rigal and Rosita Rosenberg, *Liberal Judaism: The First Hundred Years* (London: Liberal Judaism, 2004), 45–55 passim on the early years, and Edward Kessler, *A Reader in Early Liberal Judaism* (London: Vallentine Mitchell, 2004), 16–18.

[4] The hand-written texts of Cohen's sermons are in the possession of his grandson, David A. Cohen Esq. of London, who graciously made a selection relevant to the Great War available to me. They are numbered, and are identified in the first full reference by number, title, and date of delivery. The typescripts of Mattuck's sermons are in the archival collection of the Leo Baeck College Library, and are identified in the first full reference by title and date of delivery. London Metropolitan Archives also claims papers of Mattuck including sermons under their listing for Liberal Jewish Synagogue:
   http://www.nationalarchives.gov.uk/a2a/records.aspx?cat=074-lma3529&cid=2-2-14#2-2-14 (26/8/2010).

[5] Julius Jelski, *Aus grosser Zeit: Predigten Gehalten im Gotteshause der Jüdischen Reform-Gemeinde in Berlin* (Berlin: L. Lamm, 1915), especially the first four sermons, delivered in August 1914. Markus Lange has written an MA dissertation on this collection under my supervision, submitted to the KCL-LBC MA Programme in Jewish Studies, 2009.

[6] For a preliminary study of this comparative dimension, see Janet Darley, 'When Europe Went to War: Jewish Sermons at the Beginning of World War One,' MA dissertation (King's College London, 2009).

As members of a nation who pray in every service for Universal Peace, the terrible clash of arms which now shatters the harmony of so large and important a section of humanity must cause us the deepest anguish. As the Kingdom of Priests... this military fever which has swept over Europe means for us a serious set-back for the ideals towards which we desire mankind to strive.[7]

A month and a half later, preaching on Rosh Hashanah, Israel Mattuck struck a similar chord. The disastrous toll in human life, 'the hearts and homes crushed and shattered by its titanic blows,' justify condemning the war as a 'great evil'. But the deeper significance makes it even worse:

The many slow achievements of human civilization not alone in physical institutions but in moral ideals are consumed by [the war] as paper in the fire. Ideals of social justice, universal peace and the improvement of man have in their realization been further removed from us. The results of centuries of human effort in civilization are threatened with complete destruction. The ruin of towns and sacred houses is but symbolic of the deeper spiritual ruin which this war threatens.[8]

Two weeks later, preaching on Sukkot, he returned to this theme: 'We feel keenly the burden of evil under which humanity is tottering. The fruits of many ages of civilization are in part ruined and in part threatened with ruin.'[9] And half a year later, preaching on 'The Meaning of Progress,' Mattuck recalled these emotions at the beginning of the war:

When the war broke out and often since, many of us asked, and heard others ask the question, 'Where is now that progress of which we boasted?'... In the presence of a great cataclysm which threatens almost to engulf our civilization, and with which are associated signs of what might almost be called a return to savagery, the idea of progress seems to be emptied of all content and the belief in it seems as a dream with which we have been deluding ourselves these many years.[10]

Any belief in the inevitability of progress now appeared naïvely misguided. The conclusion drawn by Cohen on August 8 is powerfully sobering: 'We realise that the civilisation of which we were wont to be so proud is a hollow sham, it is superficial and below the surface primitive savagery still survives'.[11]

A second, related theme is that of disillusion, not just at the reality of war but also at its causes. Later on, there would be claims that the war was being fought for great ideals and principles, but at this early stage, before the German invasion of Belgium, these ideals were not obvious. In his first sermon following England's entry into the war, Cohen adamantly insists that no great principle was at stake in the present conflict:

---

[7] Abraham Cohen, 78, 'The European Crisis', 8 August 1914, 1. Compare the similar sentiments in a sermon delivered by Morris Joseph of the Reform West London Synagogue on 15 August 1914: 'It is a terrifying paradox, a cruel blow to our most cherished ideals. It makes us doubt the value, the reality of our civilization, the stability of righteousness, the fixity of purpose of God himself', cited in Marc Saperstein, *Jewish Preaching in Times of War, 1800–2001* (Oxford: Littman Library 2008), 299–300.

[8] Israel Mattuck, 'The Comprehension of the Reality in Life', Rosh Hashanah, 21 September 1914, 5. The 'ruin of town and sacred houses' undoubtedly alludes to the devastation of Louvain with its medieval treasures at the end of August, and the German bombardment of the Rheins Cathedral just two days before the sermon was delivered.

[9] Mattuck, 'The Abiding Goodness of God', 5 October 1914, 1. Mattuck again characterized the war as 'evil' in his 28 November 1914 sermon, 'What Can Religion Do?', 3: '[W]ar is a denial of the teachings of religion. It is an evil resulting from human causes'.

[10] Mattuck, 'The Meaning of Progress', 5 February 1915, 2.

[11] Cohen, 8 August 1914, 2.

To the really religious soul – whether Jewish or Christian – the events of the past fortnight can only bring utter disgust... Conduct is considered perfectly fair in international matters which, if performed by an individual in his private affairs, would gain for him the reputation of being a liar, a rogue, a thief, and a blackguard... [The European war is] caused by the greed and selfish ambition of one, or two, nations. The desire for territorial expansion is at the root of the present upheaval. What should we think of a man who was prepared to sacrifice the lives of thousands in order to enrich himself? Yet, the parallel is very close.[12]

Toward the end of his sermon, he makes this point even more explicitly: the war has been caused by the ambitions of Russia and Germany to become the master-power of Europe, 'Therefore this war is a corrupt war, there being no high principle at stake'.[13]

In his Rosh Hashanah 1914 sermon, Mattuck presented a similar analysis of the causes of the current conflict: 'Because power has taken the place of peace, and the pursuit of wealth supplanted the pursuit of righteousness and militarism destroyed morality, we are visited with this curse'.[14] The following year, preaching on Rosh Hashanah 1915, Mattuck again looked back at the rampant confusion in a period before what he called the true issues and ideals had been clarified:

When last year we met on these days for our worship we were still dazed by the stunning force of the almost sudden blow. We saw the causes reaching far back into history and rising out of the moral and spiritual faults in human character. The causes then, perhaps, absorbed our interest to the almost complete exclusion of thoughts about the issues. Vaguely and generally we apprehended the latter. But the year has made them clear.[15]

Yet he still feels the need to repudiate the cynical view that the war is being fought for narrow national interests:

In the minds of many, a country's dominion may stand for nothing more than extended opportunities for trade, protection in various quarters of the globe, and satisfactory opportunities for them born with it to progress in industry or other material interest...

If that were all nationality stood for, then this war were a horrible and inexpiable crime, not only for the nations that brought it on, but for all the nations that partake in it. If the struggle were for trade interests, colonial possessions or mere physical power, then every drop of blood spilt in it were an eternal cry of condemnation, and every sacrifice made but as the sacrifices to unheeding idols.[16]

It is almost as if he accepts the more the idealistic approach to the war because the consequences of denying it would be so devastating.

Up to this point, almost everything I have cited could have been said by a liberal Christian priest or pastor as well. But British Jewish leaders felt an especially deep ambivalence in the alliance of their country with Czarist Russia against Germany and Austria, with their records regarding Jews so superior to that of the Russian Empire. Cohen begins his August 8 sermon noting,

Possibly at this very moment, Jew may be fighting Jew. Is it not a tragedy that our brethren by the thousands are jeopardising their lives in defence of a country like Russia which, in time of peace,

---

[12] Ibid., 2–3.

[13] Ibid., 7.

[14] Mattuck, 21 September 1914, 6.

[15] Mattuck , 'The War and Spiritual Progress', Rosh Hashanah, 9 September 1915, 2.

[16] Ibid., 8.

denies them the elementary rights of citizenship, crushes them under a burden of restrictive laws, and even permits their wholesale massacre![17]

As I have shown in a different context,[18] the ambivalence about siding with Russia was alleviated by reports of the wave of patriotism that swept over Russian Jewry, noted by Mattuck on 23 January 1915, when he said that the Russian Jews 'who themselves had suffered these horrors [of persecution] were prepared to forget them and to sacrifice their all for the country which, in spite of its past treatment, they still love'.[19] The massive number of Jews who volunteered for military service in the Czarist army, and widely-reported citations for bravery in combat, led to the expectations that their demonstration of loyalty would eventually discredit antisemites and result in the removal of discriminatory legislation. But the first theme – that Jews were fighting other Jews in unprecedented numbers – remained a cause of deep distress, especially for the Zionists.[20]

Nevertheless, in his second sermon following Britain's entry into the war, Cohen asserted strongly that Jews had a special stake and responsibility to demonstrate their loyalty to their country. British Jews 'cannot remain indifferent to the gigantic contest in which England was forced to take a part', he insists. All over Europe, Jews are being put to the test: to refute or confirm the accusations of the antisemites.

> This war will prove whether our traducers are correct who say we are self-seekers, parasites, who absorb all we can get but give nothing or little in return. Jewry has now a supreme opportunity of refuting that slander once for all, by showing that we do understand what gratitude is to a State which grants us liberty, security, and full political rights and we are prepared to make sacrifices in its time of need.[21]

In addition to enlisting in the army, Cohen urges Jews to avoid panic-driven hoarding, create opportunities for employment, give generously to charity funds, and volunteer for personal service to such organizations as the Ladies Guilds making garments for the destitute. [22]

In early 1915, Mattuck, preaching on 'War and the Jews', spoke of the hopes for the improvement of the Jewish condition in Czarist Russia because of the sacrificial devotion of Jews to the Russian national cause and the suffering of Jewish communities that bore the brunt of the battle during the first months. In the same sermon he emphasized the need to cultivate a sense of national unity, fostering a concern on the part of western Jews,

---

[17] Cohen, 8 August, 1914, 1.

[18] See Saperstein, *Jewish Preaching in Times of War, 1800–2001*, 303–4, and at greater length in 'Western Jewish Perceptions of Russian Jews at the Beginning of the First World War', *European Judaism* 43:1 (2010), 116–27.

[19] Mattuck, 'War and the Jews', 23 January 1915, 3.

[20] For a strong early expression of this view, note Rabbi Dr Samuel Daiches, speaking on 3 August 1914 at the convention of the Order of Ancient Maccabæans in Liverpool: 'On this very day nearly half a million of our brethren in the various armies of Europe are ready to fight against and kill one another, and are ready to lay down their lives. For what? Not for Palestine. Not for Jerusalem. Not for national independence. Not for Jewish supremacy, and not for the good of humanity; but in order to help the European nations to call down a curse on their own heads and to make Europe into a heap of ashes. This illustrates the depth of a tragedy in the life of the Jewish nation.' *Jewish Chronicle*, 7 August 1914, 13. And cf. also George (Gedaliah) Silverstone, in Washington DC on 25 October, 1914: 'For *we* are not fighting for our country, as is the Russian army, which is fighting for Russia, and the British army for their country, England, and the German army for Germany, and similarly the French and the Turks. Not us. We Jews are compelled to fight for all of these, not for ourselves' (Saperstein, *Jewish Preaching in Times of War*, 306–7).

[21] Cohen, 79, 'The European Crisis – II', 15 August 1914, 2–3.

[22] Ibid. 4–6.

expressed through a 'trans-national organization', to act on behalf of the Jews suffering in the East.[23]

No preacher could avoid speaking about the theological crisis presented by the war. Cohen addressed this directly in a sermon entitled 'God and the War', delivered on 24 October 1914. The question has forced itself upon many: 'What is God doing while His earth is being drenched with human blood? Why does He permit these horrors to go on? Why does He not put an end to them?' Not unexpectedly, Cohen responds that God's creation of human beings as free agents precludes divine intervention to prevent humans from carrying out their nefarious plans. Perhaps more surprising, he asserts that it would be a disaster if God intervened to stop the war at present while the root causes of the war remained unabated. And thirdly he points to some of the positive results of the war: acts of heroism and self-sacrifice, splendid examples of charity and renunciation.

Despite the challenges raised by the contemporary reality, Cohen affirms belief in a traditional providential theology: 'I am perfectly sure that God not only is aware of all that is happening but is shaping the destiny of the human race'. This is followed by a passage of powerful optimism about the regeneration of the human spirit resulting from the war's termination, using traditional images of messianic birth pangs and the dark night before the dawn. The present war

> will bring about a complete regeneration of the human race, the birth of a new humanity purged of the vices which corrupted the old. But as with the birth of the individual, the birth of the new humanity must necessarily be a time of pain and strain... Darkness does indeed enshroud us; but [future generations] will refer to it as the night which was the herald of a beautiful dawn, a dawn which brought to mankind the blessings of peace and brotherhood.[24]

Though in retrospect this appears almost painfully naïve and ironic, and Cohen would indeed become somewhat disillusioned about the capacity for regeneration as the war dragged on, the faith of the preacher may have been perceived at the time as a source of comfort and reassurance.

Mattuck articulated similar challenges to faith. On 24 April 1915, he refers to the theological test presented by the devastation of war, noting that he has already discussed this theme in the past.[25] The agonizing problem is articulated in a single sentence from his sermon on Yom Kippur morning, 1915: 'Why has God permitted so great an evil to come into the world?'[26] His responses to this challenge are in some ways similar to that of Cohen. First, he shifts responsibility away from God and onto human beings, bestowed with freedom of choice: War is 'an evil resulting from human causes... The responsibility for the evil naturally lies upon them with whom it originated.'[27] Second, he emphasizes the positive by-products of the devastation, which may in some sense serve to counter-balance the negatives, though without altering the evil of war itself. These include an enhanced sense of national

[23] Mattuck, 'War and the Jews', 23 January 1915, 3, 7.

[24] Cohen, 98, 'God and the War', 24 October 1914, 1–2, 5–7. Compare the use of this night and dawn imagery, using an aggadah about Adam's experience of the first night, by Chief Rabbi Joseph Hertz on 1 January 1916: Saperstein, *Jewish Preaching in Times of War*, 320.

[25] Mattuck, 'Some Religious Ideals and the War', 24 April 1915, 3–4.

[26] Mattuck, Yom Kippur Morning, 17 September 1915, 14. Cf. Cohen, 'When we look at the map and see the vast stretches of territory in the possession of the enemy, we grow despondent and ask despairingly, "What is God doing?" ' 183, Intercession Sermon, 1 January, 1916, 7.

[27] Mattuck, 'What Can Religion Do?' 28 November 1914, 3.

social unity and interdependence, transcending the self-interest of special social units,[28] and 'the heroism and self-sacrifice of the men in the fighting-line, the fortitude and humble resignation of those who at home bear their part of the burden',[29] and finally the challenge and opportunity of sharing in the creation of a new world which will follow the termination of the present bloodshed. Though these qualities cannot compensate for the evil, they may, to some extent, mitigate it.[30]

What then is the proper role of prayer in the context of the catastrophic bloodbath in the heart of Europe? Is it acceptable to invoke God's favour when armies are arrayed with the purpose of devastating each other? What should we be asking for? How significant is the recognition that in the churches and synagogues of the enemy nations, many people are beseeching God in the sincere belief that right is on their side? These questions were raised by the first Day of National Prayer and Intercession during the war, proclaimed by the Crown for 2 January 1915.

In his Birmingham sermon on that day, Abraham Cohen begins with a strong assertion of the traditional Jewish doctrine of God's sovereign mastery over historical events, which he presents as a doctrine intrinsic to the concept of a day of National Prayer. He concedes the challenges to this doctrine presented by the war, 'when blood is being spilt like water, when the fairness of fields is marred by trenches filled with men whose savage passions have been aroused, when murder is organised on a gigantic scale.' Furthermore, he reminds his listeners that 'the places of worship in enemy lands are also full of men and women praying to the same God for victory to their side. We believe conscientiously that we have entered into this awful struggle with clean hands and in a righteous cause; but so do our enemies.'[31]

What then is the proper spirit for this day? What follows strikes me as an extraordinary passage for a day when patriotic spirit and denigration of the enemy was being aroused in many pulpits. Our role on this day, the preacher says, is

> to commit our cause to God, even as our hostile neighbours do, and let Him decide the right. We should pray to Him not for victory but for the vindication of the truth. If justice be with us, then let our enemies be punished for the incalculable harm they have inflicted upon the human race. If justice be with them, then let God exact the penalty from us. Should both sides have contributed to the causes of this deadly struggle, we must pray to Him to let us see where we have been wrong, in what we have been guilty. [32]

We once saw war as glamorous, manly, and heroic, the preacher says. 'But now we see it in all its hideous reality, in its grim nakedness, and the sight is too ghastly to contemplate. Modern warfare is a contest of machines for killing and maiming the largest number. Those machines,

---

[28] Mattuck, 'The War and Social Conscience', 24 October 1914, 6.

[29] Mattuck, 28 November 1914, 3.

[30] Mattuck, 'Faith and the National Crisis', 2 January 1915, 3–4, 8.

[31] Cohen, 109, Intercession Sermon, 2 January 1915, 3. He would return to this reminder two years later: 'But let us not overlook the obvious fact that, in enemy lands, similar prayers are being offered to the same God for success to their cause, which they sincerely believe to be as righteous as we believe ours to be. How can God answer a petition for victory from opposing sides?' (261, 'Terrible Things in Righteousness', 30 December 1916, 5). Consciously or not, Cohen's insistence that both sides to the conflict were sincerely praying for God's help with conviction in the righteousness of their cause echoes Abraham Lincoln's Second Inaugural address during the American Civil War: the North and the South both 'read the same Bible and pray to the same God, and each invokes His aid against the other. . . . The prayers of both could not be answered'. *Abraham Lincoln: Speeches and Writings, 1859–1865* (New York: Library of America, 1989), 686–687.

[32] Cohen, 2 January 1915, 3–4.

when once silenced, must be silenced for ever and consigned to a museum as a memorial of a barbaric age which can never recur.' That is the only prayer fitting for this occasion.[33]

On the same day, the message of Liberal Rabbi Israel Mattuck on this point was quite similar to that of his Orthodox Colleague in Birmingham. No country may assume that all right is on its side. We are firm in the belief that we are fighting for the triumph of justice and right, he insists. Nevertheless,

> It is true that human judgments may be wrong, and what we conceive to be right may not be so. And therefore we must be humble even while determined and confident, and avoid self-righteousness even while struggling for that which we conceive to be righteousness. It is for man to seek guidance through his faith and work by the best light he has. If then he err, God's mercy has prepared forgiveness for him.[34]

In his Intercession sermon a year later, Cohen reiterated his faith in divine providence. The very idea of an Intercession service is dependent upon the belief that God can, and does, interfere in the schemes of mankind – otherwise prayers addressed to Him are vain and useless. Yet he recognizes that similar beliefs could be documented on the other side:

> The Germans have that faith in abundance. If the reports of speeches attributed to the Kaiser are correct, we see that his belief that God interferes in the activities of men and nations is very real indeed, so real that he claims the Deity to be an ally of Germany. That is gross profanation, and we must beware lest *we* claim Him as an ally of Great Britain. In the victory of Germany or England, as political States, I believe God to be entirely unconcerned. But I do most firmly believe that God is concerned in the defeat of wickedness and treachery and evil ambition. If righteousness were to succumb finally–I emphasize that word 'finally'–to the onslaught of brute force, my faith in God would be shattered. But as I scan the pages of the past, I read distinctly the lesson that right has always triumphed eventually, and I believe that this lesson will receive its culminating illustration in the present time of crisis.[35]

And so he concludes, in the spirit of his statement from the previous year, 'On this Sabbath of Intercession all that we should do is to commit our cause to God and let Him decide the right. We should pray to Him, not so much for victory, as for the vindication of truth. And above all, we should supplicate Him to hasten the end of this dreadful deluge of blood... .'[36]

One year later, at the third intercession sermon, the challenges to faith had not become any less pressing for Cohen. With courageous candour, he reviews the progression of events and their psychological toll during two and a half years of combat:

> But does God hear prayer? I put the question bluntly, because I fear that at the back of our minds we have doubts about it, doubts which have probably been strengthened by the devastating storm through which we are passing.[37]

Here the preacher is articulating questions and doubts on behalf of his congregants, suggesting that he too may not be immune to them. He then proceeds to specifics, in a passage suggesting that he too was not immune to bewilderment:

---

[33] Ibid., 4.

[34] Mattuck, 2 January 1915, 5. Compare A.A. Green's strong challenge to the very institution of the Day of National Prayer in his Intercession Sermon the following year (1 January 1916): A.A. Green, *Sermons*, ed. Henrietta Adler (London: Martin Hopkinson, 1935), 135–41.

[35] Cohen, Intercession Sermon, 1 January 1916, 6.

[36] Ibid., 8.

[37] Cohen, Intercession Service, 30 December 1916, 1.

Six months after the outbreak of war, we held an Intercession Service and called upon God to aid the right. It was followed by a year's hard fighting, the end of which found the enemy in a stronger position than before. Russia, our great hope, had been forced to retreat. Poland and Serbia were completely overrun; Bulgaria had declared against us. We held another Intercession Service, and few of us at that time doubted that before another twelve months had elapsed, our cause would have been won. But we have had to endure bitter disappointments. Our men fought like the heroes they are; they made the supreme sacrifice in appalling numbers; but the resources of the enemy proved still too strong. Victory is a long way off; even the entry of Roumania on our side has turned out a disaster... Why then hold an intercession Service? Does God heed our supplications?'[38]

Unlike Cohen, Mattuck does not defend the traditional idea of God's sovereign control over historical events, probably because he did not believe in it – this is indeed a significant theological difference between the two preachers. The sceptical position is expressed perhaps most clearly by Mattuck in a sermon delivered on 5 January 1918, the fifth annual National Day of Prayer during the war. What may we pray for on this day? he asks rhetorically? 'There are some who still look to God for relief from human burdens, responsibilities and duties, hoping that He would do things for us. The day of miraculous interference by Providence in the course of human events is past. What we want, we must ourselves strive for. For our failures we must ourselves pay; and for the failures and sins of the race, all humanity must pay.'[39] Here Mattuck follows the standard liberal response to the theological challenge: God is not responsible for the war, it is the failure of human beings. *We* are the ones who must take responsibility. Nevertheless, in his sermon following the Armistice, on 16 November 1918, he invokes some of the traditional rhetoric of divine providence:

With gratitude we greet the coming of victory and peace, gratitude to God Whose guiding hand lies on the events in human history, from Whom alone comes the strength men use. Even as we prayed to Him and stayed our hearts on Him when things seemed to go ill for this country and those associated with it, and the deep darkness of anxiety brooded over our spirits, so now that light has shined forth let us see in it the flashings of God's arm and in all humility praise and thank Him.[40]

One of the important themes in all war-time sermons is the way the preacher speaks about the enemy. Does he resort to the kind of disparaging language that is prevalent in the general society: 'the Hun is at the gate'? Does he demonize the enemy as the embodiment of evil: the Amalek of the present time? Or does he recognize a common human bond on both sides of the battleground?

Abraham Cohen avoids the most derogatory rhetoric in speaking about those whom he characterizes as 'the enemy'. As we have already seen, Cohen recognized that genuine and heartfelt religious faith can be found in the churches and synagogues of the opposing side: 'in enemy lands, similar prayers are being offered to the same God for success to their cause, which they sincerely believe to be as righteous as we believe ours to be'.[41] His purpose in such passages is to undermine a self-righteous sense of entitlement in claims to God's favour.

---

[38] Ibid., 1–2.

[39] Mattuck, 'Looking to God', 5 January 1918, 2.

[40] Mattuck, 'Victory and Peace', Thanksgiving Service, 16 November 1918, 1.

[41] Cohen, Intercession Sermon, 30 December 1916, 5. Cf. the passage cited above from the Intercession Sermon two years previously: 'We believe conscientiously that we have entered into this awful struggle with clean hands and in a righteous cause; but so do our enemies.'

At times he gives the Germans a somewhat grudging respect. In a Hanukkah sermon from December 1914, he conceded the discipline and technical prowess of the German soldier, in order to apply the Hanukkah theme of triumph not by might but by the power of the spirit:

> The German Army as a war machine has been brought to the highest pitch of perfection... As an army and from the military standpoint, there is nothing to equal it in the world. But it is an iron image with feet of clay, and is going to be smashed to pieces. It lacks one thing which will bring about its downfall – it lacks the true moral spirit. That was shown conclusively at the Battle of Mons in the month of August... The spirit of our men proved mightier than the superior numbers of the enemy.[42]

Yet Cohen was also capable of condemning the policies and practice of German warfare, the soldiers who executed them, and the population which supported them. His Intercession Day sermon from January 1915 includes a prayer that God may soften the hearts of the adversaries towards those opposed to them. What follows, however, is a strong condemnation, if not of the German soldiers themselves, then certainly of their behaviour. The enemy, he says,

> seem to have retained the old savage practice of war. They are fighting like barbarians, not like a European nation in the 20th century. They have deliberately adopted the policy of *Schrecklichkeit* – the policy of 'terrorism', their hope being to strike fear in the heart of their opponents. Accordingly they have heartlessly overrun Belgium, laid its towns in ruins, shockingly ill-treated the civilian population; they have dropped bombs indiscriminately, and a few weeks ago crowned their work by bombarding undefended coast towns, killing inoffensive women and children. What is most deplorable about the matter is the fact that these contraventions of international law have been applauded by the entire German people.[43]

Mattuck goes considerably further in insisting on the humanity of the enemy. In a sermon delivered on 28 November 1914, he raises a classical problem for Jewish leaders preaching in times of war: the tendency to exult in a military victory while ignoring the human costs for those who were defeated.[44] 'We want our country's arms to be victorious, and the victory of one combatant must mean the defeat of another. Can we not, however, spare a tear for the fallen in the opposing host? Certainly there can be no ground for full-hearted rejoicing.'

The preacher continues by citing a celebrated passage from the rabbinic aggadah: When the waters of the Red Sea closed over the Egyptian army, the heavenly angels began to sing a song of praise for the Almighty. God immediately rebuked them, saying, *Ma'asei yadai tov'im ba-yam, ve-atem omrim shirah?* 'My creatures are drowning in the sea, and you would sing a song of praise?!' or as Mattuck translates it, 'Will ye sing a song of praise when so many of my children have been destroyed?' (The extent to which this passage appears in war-time sermons is a touchstone for the liberalism of the speaker.) What follows is a strong critique of the contemporary discourse of victory, 'The talk about 'crushing' the adversary becomes but a stumbling block in the way of peace, and a menace to its continuance after it is established.

---

[42] Cohen, 106, 'The Invincible Spirit', 13 December 1914, 4–5.

[43] Cohen, 2 January 1915, 6–7.

[44] For this theme in the middle of the eighteenth century, see Marc Saperstein, *'Your Voice Like a Ram's Horn'* (Cincinnati: HUC Press, 1996), 151–52.

False ideals must be crushed, unrighteousness must be trampled under foot, but nations and men must be helped to a realization of what is good, and to a horror of what is evil.'[45]

Mattuck's refusal to demonize the enemy, to set them outside the circle of human empathy and concern, continued through the war, as we see in his sermon delivered on a National Day of Prayer, 5 January 1918: 'Today we think altogether of the life of the nation, and of our own lives in relation to it. And may we not say we think of the life of humanity, yes, of *foes* as of friends? That the right we seek, as God has given us to see that right, is for the world?'[46] Here we see the universalistic instinct of the Liberal asserting itself despite the bleak realities of his time.

This same instinct is expressed in occasional strong responses to the less appealing emotions evident within the broader society. Speaking on 23 October 1915, Mattuck states that in addition to the admirable emotions of national solidarity and self-sacrifice, he recognizes that the war has stirred up base emotions, opposed to the spirit of true religion: 'There has, for example, been an outcry for reprisals for the dastardly murders of women and children committed by the airships. It is not likely that such reprisals can serve any useful military purpose... [They] can have no value, but the satisfaction of the desire for revenge, and great as the temptation here might be, we are yet commanded by religion to seek no vengeance'. And even if they *had* a distinct military benefit, they would still not be justifiable, the preacher insists.[47]

In his National Day of Prayer sermon for 5 January 1918, Mattuck asserts that a grave danger to the national life arises from 'those who exalt the passions of war, as hatred, the lust for revenge, and from those who would translate the hope of victory into hopes for material gain. Only the other day we were all invited to take part in an organized campaign to spread hatred... The effort to conceal the true character of the clamour for passions under the cloak of patriotism can deceive no one who wishes to see.'[48]

Mattuck returns to this theme in a special service held on 3 August 1918, the fourth anniversary of Britain's entry into the war. Alongside the positive elements he acknowledges both on the fields of battle and in the spiritual realm – the greater emphasis on moral and spiritual values rather than merely self-defence and national self-determination, the renewed faith in democracy, the League of Nations – there is a debit side: the intensifying spirit of hatred and vengeance. 'If it were not disgusting, it would be heartbreaking, to see how innocent people are harassed and persecuted only to satisfy the outbursts of a blind passion

---

[45] Mattuck, 28 November 1914, 7–8. This would appear to be a characteristically liberal stance. There was, however, a disparity among the leaders of British Liberal Judaism. My colleague Daniel Langton has called to my attention a letter written to Mattuck by Claude G Montefiore, which states, 'Again, for instance, there is a rumour tonight that a German battleship has been sunk. I rejoice. . . . Even if all have gone down, I rejoice that there is one German battleship less.' Unfortunately the letter is undated, and it could be totally independent of the sermon. On the other hand, it is certainly not impossible that Mattuck chose to make this point and cite this aggadah about 'My creatures are drowning in the sea' as an explicit response to the letter and the attitude it reflects. It is also possible that Montefiore wrote the letter in response to this sermon. Such are the fascinating ambiguities of working with this literature. See Daniel Langton, *Claude Montefiore: His Life and Thought* (London: Vallentine Mitchell, 2002), 9, with reference on 22.

[46] Mattuck, 'Looking to God', 5 January 1918, 1.

[47] Mattuck, 'The Challenge to Religion in War', 23 October 1915, 10–11.

[48] Mattuck, 5 January 1918, 5–6. The reference to the 'organized campaign to spread hatred', which everyone in the congregation would probably have understood, is unclear to me.

which parades as patriotism. It is unworthy at any time, but worse in a nation giving its best in a war for righteousness.'[49]

As the war continued beyond all expectations at its outset, neither preacher was able to remain naïvely optimistic about the fulfilment of the hope that this would be 'the war which will end war'.[50] A generation later, preaching almost two years after the beginning of the Second World War, Cohen cited a passage from a sermon he delivered in 1917, which appears to be hauntingly prophetic:

> Not the crushing of Germany and the perpetuation of the evil which brought this war into being should be the aim; for in that case, all this precious blood will have been spilt in vain. What must be crushed is the survival of barbaric methods which have brought disaster upon the world. Merely to replace one self-hypnotized War Lord by another is to prepare for another European war. Should – as we hope and pray – should victory side with us and our allies, and should the result be just a weakened Germany and another competition in armaments and another race for power – then we shall have fought in vain, and the struggle will with certainty recur.[51]

Nor was Mattuck unduly sanguine about the prospects that the values of national self-determination, justice, and peace would actually be achieved once the war had ended. In certain passages, Mattuck seems to have had an uncanny unease about the future, his great hope mingled with concern about possible perils at the conclusion of the war. In a sermon delivered 9 December 1916, he warned that historical precedents were not encouraging about the prospects for the war to transform a society for the good. The precedent he cites was from his own history across the Atlantic:

> The greatest war in the last century, and one which has been referred to again and again in connection with the present war as a sort of parallel, the American Civil War, holds out both a promise and a warning. While it produced the actual aims for which it was fought in spite of the great odds against which Lincoln and his associates had to contend and the early discouraging defeats, it was, however, followed by a period of great confusion and what was worse, the play of some of the worst passions. It has taken America many decades to overcome the evil of the period of reconstruction which followed the civil war, and perhaps that evil is not yet altogether overcome.[52]

Although spoken from his education as an American, that final formulation – 'perhaps that evil is not yet altogether overcome' – is a fine example of British understatement.

On 19 January 1918, Mattuck warned against the sentiment of conceptualizing reconstruction as an attempt 'to produce in the nation a greater military efficiency for the next time when its military prowess may be challenged'. Continuing to strengthen military capacity in order to meet a possible future threat was to adopt the militaristic philosophy of the German state and the society against which Britain was fighting. Of course, the logical

---

[49] Mattuck, 'After Four Years', 3 August 1918, 6. This passage is extremely close in sentiment to the sermon delivered by the Orthodox Rabbi Herman Gollancz a month later on Rosh Hashanah 1918 in a sermon entitled 'Nationalism Within Bounds'. Saperstein, *Jewish Preaching in Times of War*, 370–73.

[50] Cohen identified H.G. Wells as the one who originated the phrase (in August 1914), which became quite popular, based on the assumption that the hideous destructiveness would convince all reasonable people that war is 'unspeakably loathsome', but by May 1916, he notes that the phrase was no longer heard so frequently, due to doubts that this argument from experience would be enough to make future war inconceivable: See Cohen, 288, 'The Cause of War', 19 May 1916, 1.

[51] Cohen, 80, 'The Worship of Molech', 23 August, 1941. I have not found the original text of this sermon.

[52] Mattuck, 'The War and Character', 9 December 1916, 6.

consequence of this anti-militaristic vision of post-war reconstruction was that Germany must be crushed to the point where she would be incapable of waging war again. Mattuck therefore rejected premature peace initiatives from Germany, citing the statement by Prime Minister David Lloyd George, so painfully ironic in retrospect, 'There must be no "next time"'.[53]

His hopes for the future were expressed in a sermon delivered some nine months later, on 7 September 1918: 'A new world, where peace shall not be but the moment of exhaustion after the war and of rest before the new war, but the abiding condition of man rooted in the love and pursuit of righteousness'. Yet the same sermon contains a warning that – also in retrospect – seems frighteningly prophetic: 'An unscrupulous or deluded demagogue with plausible tongue and violent sincerity, seeming or real, could make out of the present susceptibility to new ideas and change a spirit of evil.'[54] It is unclear to me whether in this context he was thinking of Germany or of England, but it was certainly a nightmare that he must have been devastated to see fulfilled.

To be sure, I have presented a limited sample of two preachers in one war, from the same country. But it is striking to me is how similar these pulpit messages are. The major exception was in Cohen's insistence on divine providence, despite the apparent empirical refutation posed by the war – this was a position he maintained even through World War II – and perhaps Mattuck's heightened insistence on seeing the Germans as fellow human beings. Setting aside personal style, on all the other themes relating to the war, it would be difficult to differentiate between the two men. I believe that the same would be true in comparing the war-time sermons of, let us say, the Reform Rabbi Morris Joseph and the Orthodox Rabbi Hermann Gollancz. In my judgment, these figures justify speaking of normative Judaism in the Anglo-Jewish context from the early twentieth century. I wonder whether we could pick similar examples across the divide of Orthodox and Progressive Judaism in the UK today.

BIBILIOGRAPHY

Unpublished Texts

Cohen, Abraham, 'Sermons', manuscript collection in possession of David A. Cohen, Esq.

Mattuck, Israel, 'Sermons', typescript collection in Leo Baeck College Library Archival Collection.

Published Texts

Cohen, Abraham, *An Anglo-Jewish Scrapbook, 1600–1940: The Jew Through English Eyes* (London: M. L. Cailingold, 1943).

Cohen, Abraham, *Jewish Homiletics* (London: M.L. Cailingold, 1937).

---

[53] Mattuck, 'Ideals in Reconstruction', 19 January 1918, 5. The statement was made by Lloyd George in an address at a rally on 4 August 1917 commemorating the third anniversary of the war (which received extensive front-page coverage in the New York Times, 5 August 1917, 1–2). On Mattuck's ideas about the necessary post-war reconstruction of British society, see his sermon 'The Basis for Social Reconstruction after the War', 3 February 1917, in which he argues that the state, with a truly representative government, should make decisions about education, and other critical problems, rather than leaving them to groups in accordance with special interests; it should not leave industrial relations 'to be settled by bargains, strikes and lock-outs, regulated and impelled by the interest of one group or another' (9).

[54] Mattuck, 'New Life' (Day of Memorial, Wigmore Hall), 7 September 1918, 4–5, 3.

Darley, Janet, 'When Europe Went to War: Jewish Sermons at the Beginning of World War One', MA dissertation (King's College London, 2009).

Green, A.A., *Sermons*, ed. Henrietta Adler (London: Martin Hopkinson, 1935).

Jelski, Julius, *Aus grosser Zeit: Predigten Gehalten im Gotteshause der Jüdischen Reform-Gemeinde in Berlin* (Berlin: L. Lamm, 1915).

Kessler, Edward, *A Reader in Early Liberal Judaism* (London: Vallentine Mitchell, 2004).

Lange, Markus, 'Themes, Topoi and Theologies in Dr Julius Jelski's *Aus großer Zeit*. Twelve German-Jewish Wartime Sermons from August–December 1914', MA dissertation (King's College London, 2009).

Langham, Raphael, *250 Years of Convention and Contention* (London: Vallentine Mitchell, 2010).

Langton, Daniel, *Claude Montefiore: His Life and Thought* (London: Vallentine Mitchell, 2002).

Lincoln, Abraham, *Abraham Lincoln: Speeches and Writings, 1859–1865* (New York: Library of America, 1989).

Rigal, Lawrence and Rosita Rosenberg, *Liberal Judaism: The First Hundred Years* (London: Liberal Judaism, 2004).

Saperstein, Marc, *Jewish Preaching in Times of War, 1800–2001* (Oxford: Littman Library, 2006).

Saperstein, Marc, 'Western Jewish Perceptions of Russian Jews at the Beginning of the First World War', *European Judaism* 43:1 (2010), 116–27.

Saperstein, Marc, *Your Voice Like A Ram's Horn: Themes and Texts in Traditional Jewish Preaching* (Cincinnati: HUC Press, 1996).

AMBIVALENT NORMATIVITY: REASONS FOR CONTEMPORARY JEWISH DEBATE OVER THE LAWS OF WAR

George R. Wilkes*

A blossoming body of academic literature argues for a range of normative Jewish approaches to the laws of war, based on ancient or medieval texts and on the argument that there is a practical contemporary need for a distinctive Jewish approach to making war and peace. Much of this literature is motivated by the conviction that there is a normative Jewish approach, against which competing opinions can be shown to be less credible and authentic. This essay explores the ambivalence which arises as a result of the twofold awareness that the textual basis which supports competing approaches to justice and peace is not unambiguous, and that geographical, denominational and political differences distinguish the various projects for a revived Jewish norm to govern the making of war and peace.

Introduction

That Jews are perceived to lack a coherent normative approach to war has occasioned an entirely new body of literature in the last fifty years. This work, typically in essay, sermon or edited paper form, responds to a common compulsion to apply Jewish textual resources to new dilemmas posed by contemporary warfare. Many of the writers engaged in this enterprise are clearly troubled by the discordant approaches which other writers take to the normative dimension of the subject. The present essay examines the reasons for the resulting debate, and the consequent ambivalence towards normative judgements that is thereby associated with the attempt to apply Jewish law and ethics to war.

Numerically the greatest portion of these essays investigate the bases for a distinctive Jewish religious response to contemporary Israeli and American military affairs based on Jewish texts alone,[1] though a growing number also examine parallels between Jewish teachings on war and the Christian 'just war tradition'.[2] What this Jewish approach to war

---

* Research Fellow, School of Divinity, University of Edinburgh. Email: george.wilkes@ed.ac.uk

[1] For three of the most useful introductions to this work, see J. David Bleich, *Contemporary Halakhic Problems* (New York: Ktav/Yeshiva University Press, 1977–1989), Vols I–IV; Michael Walzer, ed., *Law, Politics and Morality in Judaism* (Princeton: Princeton University Press, 2006); and Murray Polner and Stefan Merken, *Peace, Justice and Jews: Reclaiming Our Tradition* (New York: Bunim & Bannigan, 2007).

[2] For example M. Broyde, 'Fighting the War and the Peace: Battlefield Ethics, Peace Talks, Treaties, and Pacifism in the Jewish Tradition' in J. Patout Burns, ed., *War and Its Discontents: Pacifism and Quietism in the Abrahamic Religions* (Washington D.C.: Georgetown University Press, 1996), 1–30; George R. Wilkes, 'Judaism and Justice in War', in Paul A. Robinson, ed., *Just War in Comparative Perspective* (Aldershot: Ashgate Press, 2003), 9–23; Norman Solomon, 'The Ethics of War in Judaism' in David Rodin and Richard Sorabji, eds., *The Ethics of War: Shared Problems in Different Traditions* (Aldershot: Ashgate Press, 2006), 108–137; Norman Solomon, 'The ethics of war in Judaism' in Torkel Brekke, ed., *The Ethics of War in Asian Civilizations: A Comparative Perspective* (Abingdon/New York: Routledge, 2006), 39–82; George R. Wilkes, 'Legitimation and Limits of War in Jewish Tradition', Mark Levene, 'Imagining Co-Existence in the Face of War: Jewish "Pacifism" and the State 1917-1948', and Melissa Raphael, 'The

consists of is as contested as are Christian just war teachings. Some versions tend to a deliberately liberal, humanistic, and even quasi-pacifist position, insisting on the utility of a tradition of Jewish norms in guarding against the whim and self-interest of those who in power seek a bloody sacrifice from their enemies and from their own citizens.[3] The idea that there is a pacific or humanistic ethic in Judaism that seeks to limit every facet of the conduct of war also has fierce opponents.[4] They argue that it is irresponsible to expose soldiers and citizens to any unnecessary risk: war is governed by the ability of one side to overwhelm its opponents, and what they see as normative Judaism recognizes that excessively 'limited' warfare creates drawn-out conflicts which may be in the long run even bloodier.[5] In this view, Judaism is not pacifist, and nor does it promote the expectation that a people will, through nobility or humility, commit collective suicide, in Michael Broyde's elegant phrase.[6]

A relatively minor irritant generating some of the clash of perspectives can be found in denominational difference. The Reform movement in the USA has since the 1960s embraced more self-declared pacifists than the Modern Orthodox have,[7] and the influence of a theological or prophetic pacifism on influential Progressive thinkers from the nineteenth century onward has irked both Orthodox and Conservative critics alike.[8] This inter-denominational debate has informed both Orthodox and non-Orthodox polemic. One of the most insightful documents showing the development of this debate is presented in the proceedings of a multi-denominational rabbinic conference on war held in New York in 1963. And yet, as the conference proceedings recurrently underlined, clashes over the use of authoritative Jewish texts also mark discussion within each denomination – indeed, much of this debate is constructed as an internal Orthodox debate, and particularly a concern of the established authorities of the National Religious community in Israel. In the polemical texts covered here, normative claims are frequently strengthened as much by generalizations about consensus as they are by assertions about the binding nature of particular commands or texts.[9] The literature written since that time gives almost as much attention to the rhetorical strategies which contribute to this renewed debate as it does to the nature of an authoritative Jewish wartime law or ethic as a subject in itself.

Gendering of Jewish Post-Holocaust Responses to War and Collective Violence' in Linda Hogan and Dylan Lehrke, eds., *Religion And The Politics Of Peace And Conflict* (Eugene OR: Wipf & Stock, 2009), 3–24, 57–82, 159–174.

[3] Polner and Merken, *Peace, Justice and Jews*; Murray Polner and Naomi Goodman, eds., *The Challenge of Shalom: The Jewish Tradition of Peace and Justice* (Philadelphia: New Society Publishers, 1994).

[4] Maurice Lamm, 'After the War – Another look at Pacifism and Selective Conscientious Objection' in Menachem Kellner, ed., *Contemporary Jewish Ethics* (New York: Sanhedrin Press, 1978), 221–238.

[5] M. Broyde, 'Fighting the War and the Peace', 1–30.

[6] Michael Broyde, 'Just Wars, Just Battles and Just Conduct in Jewish Law: Jewish Law Is Not a Suicide Pact' in Lawrence Schiffman and Joel B. Wolowelsky, eds., *War and Peace in the Jewish Tradition* (New York: Yeshiva University Press, 2007), 1–44.

[7] For a critical treatment of long-term shifts in Reform attitudes, see Judith Bleich, 'Military Service: Ambivalence and Contradiction' in Lawrence Schiffman and Joel B. Wolowelsky, eds., *War and Peace in the Jewish Tradition* (New York: Yeshiva University Press, 2007), 415–76.

[8] For example, Maurice Lamm, 'After the War' in Kellner, ed., *Contemporary Jewish Ethics*, 221–238, and Jacob Agus, 'A Jewish View of the Problem of War: Prevention Today' in *Dimensions of Peace: A Jewish Confrontation. Report of a Conference on the Relevance of Jewish Tradition to the Problems of a Nuclear Age* (New York: Dimensions of Peace, 1963), 2–4.

[9] *Dimensions of Peace: A Jewish Confrontation. Report of a Conference on the Relevance of Jewish Tradition to the Problems of a Nuclear Age* (New York: Dimensions of Peace, 1963), *passim*.

What follows is a critical commentary on selected exempla, sometimes reporting Israeli positions in order to cast light on the debate in English-language texts, often quite self-consciously engaged in a developing transnational and – for many commentators – transdenominational debate on the subject. The commentary is divided into three parts, focused on three factors which trouble assertions about Jewish laws or ethics in making war. First, the textual basis for a normative Jewish teaching about war is slim, and the impact of historical contexts makes for such a diversity of texts and opinions that many judge it difficult to arrive at any generalizations at all.[10] The same could easily be said about the Christian just war tradition, and indeed about *jihad* in Islam: passages on the subject written in the formative periods of both religions are both brief and contradictory, and subsequent innovations make the traditions ever more diverse. However, the textual evidence for a normative Jewish approach to war is fraught with obscurities for a further reason, which weakens the scope for an easy consensus between legal scholars.

This second factor is the distinctive historical relationship between Diaspora Jews and the governments under which they lived, which meant that legal scholars faced far less demand for a body of legal or ethical writings about military practice. It is commonly suggested that Jewish debate about war has been even more stunted than the Christian and Muslim traditions by the lack of power held by Jews across the last two millenia, at least until the creation of the State of Israel, and that, primarily with this in mind, the last sixty years has seen the return of a genre of writing about *halakhah* in war.[11] The claim itself demands examination: if it is accepted, then a *halakhic* or normative Jewish approach to war stands on whether or not it is of practical use for political leaders and for soldiers; not primarily on whether it creates an effective limit on power, nor on the potential offense presented by power unregulated by ethics. The second part of this essay examines the role of practical demand in the recent flowering of Jewish legal and ethical tracts on the making of war. The bulk of those who have engaged in this debate are academics, and – though the Israeli writers perform national service and reserve duty – they are not writing as serving soldiers, nor professionally involved in the military.

The third and final section addresses a set of questions about the nature of ethics, law and human purpose which underpin the quite different notions of practicality deployed by the commentators under review. While some view war as an appropriate subject for the application of a normative Jewish law or ethics, and some even treat it as the archetypal instance in which a normative Judaism is needed, others argue that war is essentially lawless, or otherwise outside the realm in which a Jewish ethic or norm can be meaningfully applied. A diverse range of essayists examine war in the light of these more foundational normative questions. In common, they suggest that Jewish texts, in all their diversity, provide a basis for reflection on this deeper level of ethical and legal obligation as rich, and therefore as useful, as can be found in any other religious tradition.

---

[10] Abraham Cronbach, 'Judaism and World Peace' in *Dimensions of Peace*, 1; Aviezer Ravitsky, 'Prohibited Wars' in Walzer, *Law, Politics and Morality in Judaism*, 169.

[11] Walzer, *Law, Politics and Morality in Judaism*, 150; Stuart A. Cohen, 'The Re-Discovery of Orthodox Jewish Laws Relating to the Military and War (*Hilkhot Tzavah U-Milchamah*) in Contemporary Israel: Trends and Implications' in *Israel Studies* 12:2 (2007), 1–28; Arye Edrei, 'Law, Interpretation, and Ideology: The Renewal of the Jewish Laws of War in the State of Israel' in *Cardozo Law Review* 28:1 (2006), 188– s227.

1. Legal text and context

The textual basis for a consistent normative approach to war is clear to some and quite obscure to other, equally insightful, commentators. To many essayists, key Biblical and post-Biblical texts constitute obvious foundations for a normative Jewish approach to war. By contrast, a second range of thinkers, Orthodox and non-Orthodox, argue that each text must be viewed in its historical context, not assimilated to some overarching external norm. That the former would naturally include some of the more committed pacifist and anti-pacifist contributors to the debate is only to be expected. Be that as it may, many of the more determinedly radical writers insist on a sophisticated separation between textual analysis and normative judgement.

Deuteronomy 20 has long been treated as a *locus classicus* for Jewish discussions of what is legitimate in war, and what illegitimate. This is its status in chapter 8 of tractate *Sotah* of the Mishnah, and subsequently in much medieval commentary on the nature of Biblical war. A summary of Deuteronomy 20 reveals a chapter which at face value provides an interesting basis for legal and ethical limit to warfare, though it is neither explicit nor definitive in identifying reasons for these limits. The Children of Israel are instructed that on going out to battle, they are not to fear; a war priest is also to counsel the people to have no fear; officers are to urge newly-weds to return home, as well as those who have just built a home or planted a vineyard; captains are to be appointed over the soldiers; the enemy should be approached with an offer of peace in return for tribute; if they refuse, it is the enemy that is making war, and a siege ensues at the end of which every male is to be killed, taking their wives, children and goods as booty; unless they be of the seven Canaanite tribes, which are to be utterly destroyed so that Israel not learn idolatry from them; and finally, fruit trees may not be felled, while other trees may be used for the siege, until – the passage ends – the city falls.

The limitations of the text alone could explain much of the unresolved debate over the nature of 'war' in Jewish circles. War is not defined, leaving the commentators quoted in the Mishnah and Talmud divided over which provisions in the chapter apply to defensive wars, which are treated as, to all intents and purposes, wars commanded by God (the *milhemet mitzvah*).[12] Some of the provisions are held to apply solely to discretionary or opportunistic wars fought against the enemies of the people at the instigation of the leaders of the Jewish people (the *milhemet reshut*, once translated as 'political wars', now commonly rendered as permitted wars, or wars launched by the authorities).[13] Jewish commentators continue to debate whether the final verses about trees describe a strictly limited and humanitarian code of military conduct, or rather a 'no-holds barred' warfare waged with one eye on military necessity and another on the moral cause for which victory must be achieved – and both approaches find support within the Mishnah, Talmud and Tosefta.[14]

Where the Mishnah and Talmud advance discussion about the definition of war in the biblical text, there is much which remains unclear. The Talmud (Sotah 44b) distinguishes

---

[12] Bleich, *Contemporary Halakhic Problems*, Vol. III, 252.

[13] One of the most insightful discussions can be found in Geoffrey B. Levey, 'Judaism and the Obligation to Die for the State' in *AJS Review* 12:2 (Autumn 1987), 175–203.

[14] See Solomon, 'The Ethics of War in Judaism' in Rodin and Sorabji, eds., *The Ethics of War*, 113, and Wilkes, 'Legitimations and Limits of War in Jewish Traditions' in Hogan and Lehrke, eds., *Religion And The Politics Of Peace And Conflict*, 21.

between the 'commanded' wars of conquest fought by Joshua and the 'discretionary' wars of conquest fought by King David. About the basic distinction between these categories J. David Bleich notes that there was no recorded Talmudic dispute, yet the exact boundaries between the precedents set for a defensive war, a pre-emptive war and a preventive war have been the subject of an 'exceedingly complex' rabbinic discussion.[15] By no stretch of the imagination is Deuteronomy 20 a summary statement of a Jewish law of war. Indeed, the most extended Mishnaic treatment of the text (in *Sotah* 8) appears as part of a debate about the use of the holy language, not about war or politics, and this chapter of the Mishnah does not cover all of the issues raised by the biblical text. One popular, if contested, reading of the Mishnaic and Talmudic texts on war construes these texts as deliberately and progressively narrowing the scope for war-making over time: the Deuteronomic mandate for 'commanded' conquest soon disappears, and by Tannaitic times the oracle required for 'political' wars had long been unavailable.[16] At the same time, the Mishnah does not present the argument, as it could have done, that the entirety of Deuteronomy 20 applied only to the original conquest of the Land. The terse statements of the Mishnah and Talmud exacerbate the difficulties of drawing a normative reading from either, as the Central Conference of American Rabbis, the principal Reform rabbinic body in North America, noted in its responsa on preventive war in 2007.[17] The most serious attempts to find a definitive and faithful interpretation on the part of Orthodox *halakhic* scholars such as J. David Bleich and Michael Broyde do not rest on a plain reading of these texts alone, but seek to find compelling interpretations through reflection on a wide range of texts and commentaries. In examining the basis for a Talmudic law governing preventive wars, Bleich finds consistency through a careful casuistic approach, reading only the most limited claims into the competing opinions recorded in the Talmudic text.[18] Broyde admits more room for divergence between *poskim*, the scholars who derive normative claims through engaging with authoritative texts and *halakhic* precedent, though compelling rationale and the consensus of succeeding generations of sages bolster his own sense of those views which are more justly called 'normative'.[19]

The elaboration of a coherent *halakhah* to apply to the making of war first received deliberate essay-length attention in the twelfth century CE, in Maimonides' *Laws of Kings and Their Wars*, the final section of his law code, the *Mishneh Torah*. Maimonides' brief survey of the biblical laws relating to kings and to 'their' wars is far from an exhaustive treatment of the biblical or Talmudic laws relating to war. Indeed, there is much in the interpretation of war given by Maimonides which diverges from the preceding textual tradition, the by-product in particular of his Islamic milieu, focussing on the prerogatives of the king, on the mandate for war to command right and forbid wrong, on the martyrdom of the soldier, and

---

[15] Bleich, *Contemporary Halakhic Problems*, Vol. III, 252.

[16] See, for example, Solomon, 'The Ethics of War in Judaism' in Rodin and Sorabji, eds., *The Ethics of War*, 110. For further discussion of Tannaitic attempts to provide restrictive interpretations of the scope for making war, see Michael S. Berger, 'Taming the Beast: Rabbinic Pacification of Second-Century Jewish Nationalism' in James K. Wellman, ed., *Belief and Bloodshed: Religion and Violence across Time and Tradition* (Lanham MD: Rowman & Littlefield, 2007), 47–62.

[17] CCAR, 'Preventive War' in CCAR Responsa (5762.8, 2007) http://data.ccarnet.org/cgi-bin/respdisp.pl?file=8&year=5762

[18] Bleich, *Contemporary Halakhic Problems*, Vol. III, 252.

[19] Broyde, 'Just Wars, Just Battles and Just Conduct in Jewish Law' in Schiffman and Wolowelsky, eds., *War and Peace in the Jewish Tradition*, 1–43, especially nn. 49, 67, 96, and 'Only the Good Die Young?' in *Me'orot* 6:1 (Shevat 5767/2006), 62-67, especially 63–64.

on the elimination of idolatry.[20] Nevertheless, the book's definitive style and relative completeness has given it a central place in rabbinic debate over the *halakhah* of war. Few commentators examining the Scriptural commandments about warfare rely on Maimonides' judgements alone,[21] though these judgements remain an unavoidable feature of scholarly and popular presentations of Jewish law and ethics in war and peace-making. Maimonides sought a clear basis for an eternally-applicable divine law, though within his own text a series of difficulties with this project become clear. Maimonides' stated argument, that there is a timeless, divinely ordained law of war, elides Deuteronomy with subsequent texts on the actions of the Prophets, Kings and Sages of Israel, and with the Mishnah, Gemara, Tosefta and Midrash. This is achieved in part by not making explicit reference to his sources, in part by selecting evidence from the latter writings, and particularly from I Samuel, where it appears to conform with Deuteronomy 20 and the surrounding Deuteronomic text devoted to the King's duties and prerogatives, beginning with Deuteronomy 17. With this in mind, his construction of the laws of war is clearly not a closely-reasoned attempt to define the historically-contingent Biblical law of war but rather a counterblast to Karaite and other heterodox arguments which separated Deuteronomic law from the laws of the Prophets and Kings of Israel, and which separated both of these again from the laws elaborated in the Mishnah and Talmud. Maimonides' bold elucidation of a normative '*halakhah* in principle' is so remote from both the Biblical text and the changing realities of war that Gerald Blidstein suggests it is wholly *aggadic* and is not an accurate representation of a normative *halakhah*.[22]

By contrast, for a scholar seeking a medieval authority on which to found a Jewish just war tradition, the *Laws of Kings and Their Wars*, and the subsequent tradition of commentaries on the work, is as coherent and encompassing in its scope as the works of his Christian and Muslim contemporaries. If the distinctiveness of Maimonides' text and context raises questions about its utility for Jewish thought about war today, there is no shortage of scholars for whom it is viewed as a usable, even a preferred, basis for a principled discussion of ethical and legal constraints on modern warfare.[23]

Against these texts, the more quietist or thoroughly pacifist voices have many other textual resources which make war appear both wrong and thoroughly un-Jewish – classically texts read from the prophetic or wisdom literature as a basis for character perfection,[24] construing war as a divine punishment, as it has been in Jewish literature since at least the composition of the text of Jeremiah.[25] The selection and interpretation of texts troubles protagonists

---

[20] Gerald Blidstein, 'Holy War in Maimonidean Judaism' in Joel Kraemer, ed., *Perspectives on Maimonides* (Oxford: Oxford University Press, 1991), 212, 215, and, for a suggestion that Maimonides may have deployed Islamic precedent for 'safe passage', too, 216. See further in George Wilkes, 'Religious War in the Works of Maimonides and the "Maimonideans": An idea and its transit across the medieval Mediterranean' in Sohail Hashmi, ed., *Just Wars, Holy Wars, and Jihads: Christian, Jewish, Muslim Encounters and Exchanges*, forthcoming.

[21] See, for example, Broyde's comments in Broyde, 'Just Wars, Just Battles and Just Conduct in Jewish Law' in Schiffman and Wolowelsky, eds., *War and Peace in the Jewish Tradition*, 13–15 and 19–20.

[22] Blidstein, 'Holy War in Maimonidean Judaism' in Kraemer, ed., *Perspectives on Maimonides*, 215.

[23] For example, David Schatz, 'Introduction', and Broyde, 'Just Wars, Just Battles and Just Conduct in Jewish Law' in Schiffman and Wolowelsky, eds., *War and Peace in the Jewish Tradition*, xiv–xv and 13–15, 19–20; Michael Walzer, *Just and Unjust Wars* (New York: Basic Books, 1977), 168.

[24] For example, Polner and Merken, *Peace, Justice and Jews*.

[25] For Josephus' debt to the precedent established in Jeremiah, for instance, see *Jewish War*, 5.402–3 and 412, 6.110, 7.453. Nicole Kelley, 'The Cosmopolitan Expression of Josephus's Prophetic Perspective in the *Jewish War*' in *Harvard Theological Review* 97:3 (2004), 257–74, especially 260.

in the debate from all perspectives, a point underlined, for instance, throughout the multidenominational rabbinic conference held in New York in 1963.[26] 'Scriptural quotations are not arguments', Abraham Cronbach, one of the leading Reform pacifists of the time, noted, 'they are embellishments'.[27] The recurrent debate over the following decades has similarly pitted two polar argumentative extremes against each other, a 'Left' and a 'Right', differentiated not by texts or interpretations used, nor by their views of legitimate chains of authority, denominational cohesion or the nature of consensus. A more important dimension of the divergence between protagonists lies in their assessment of the nature of a Jewish approach to war that has a practical impact and is coherent.

2. *Power, powerlessness and the problem of identifying practical norms*

It is a cliché that Jewish discussion of practical military ethics is limited because for two millennia Jews have not had power. For this reason, too, it is commonly concluded that there has not been the practical necessity to develop laws of war. In this period, Christian and Muslim scholars turned their attention to practical issues associated with the justification for wars, with the limits of justifiable conduct in war, and with related religious issues such as the propriety of carrying copies of the Bible or Quran into enemy territory. Jews, it is said, did not have to face these issues until the establishment of the State of Israel in 1948.[28]

The resulting picture is a caricature which glosses over a wealth of theoretical and practical reflection relating to war throughout the past two millenia. Jews have been involved in warfare throughout their history, and this has been reflected in communal organization as well as *halakhic*, homiletic and exegetical literature. It is true that there were very few dedicated publications or practical manuals of the type that informed Christian and Muslim military instruction – Israel Meir Kagan's book for Jewish soldiers in the Russian army being the most notable exception before the twentieth century.[29] The key features of the Jewish textual tradition have instead been taught through Bible and Talmud study, through sermons, through historical scholarship, and as part of broader *halakhic* and textual studies. Israeli approaches to the idea that there are Jewish norms of war were thus not created *ex nihilo*. They are adduced in the context of competing intellectual trends: democratic and nationalist, liberal and more recently post-modern, and religious.[30]

---

[26] *Dimensions of Peace: A Jewish Confrontation. Report of a Conference on the Relevance of Jewish Tradition to the Problems of a Nuclear Age* (New York: Dimensions of Peace, 1963).

[27] Cronbach, 'Judaism and World Peace', *Dimensions of Peace*, 1

[28] For example Arye Edrei, 'Divine Spirit and Physical Power: Rabbi Shlomo Goren and the Military Ethic of the Israel Defense Forces' in *Theoretical Inquiries in Law* 7/1 (January 2006), especially 255–256. David Biale's compelling work *Power and Powerlessness in Jewish History* gives a critical account of the assumption that Jews have been powerless in the Diaspora, and yet gives the subject relatively little attention, and ceases to treat questions relating to the uses of military power after the Middle Ages. David Biale, *Power and Powerlessness in Jewish History* (New York: Schocken Books, 1986).

[29] Israel Meir Kagan (commonly referred to as the Chafetz Chaim), *Mahane Yisrael*, Vilna, c. 1880 (reprinted New York: Shulsinger Brothers, 1943). For further discussion of Kagan's contribution and on subsequent halakhic literature for soldiers, see Chaniel Nahari, 'The Development of Halakhic Literature for Soldiers from 1880–1975,' Bar-Ilan University, MA thesis, 2003, especially 8–19.

[30] See, for example, Schiffman and Wolowelsky, eds., *War and Peace in the Jewish Tradition*, passim.

As careful as Bleich, Broyde and their Orthodox colleagues are to examine the *halakhic* corpus in its own terms, the material on war developed within the National Religious camp is no less marked by these modern ideologies. Eugene Korn judges that a *halakhic* approach to contemporary warfare must be supplemented by both normative and empirical calculations which are external to *halakhah* – determined by frameworks beyond *halakhic* sources and distinctively *halakhic* methodology.[31] As a result of this modern political environment, religious Zionist texts abound which debate the relative prerogatives of the government and parliament in relation to the earlier *halakhic* material on the roles of the king and Sanhedrin, material which is found both within more liberal, academic circles, and amongst the more anti-liberal streams of *yeshiva* scholars inspired by elder and younger Kooks.[32]

At the same time, the growth of a variety of types of *halakhic* publication on war in the State of Israel clearly reflects a different experience and expectation about the relationship between power and religion in the State. There is a new body of literature on general *halakhic* practice in military life, which often only implicitly or tangentially overlaps with the *halakhic* material on broader questions of military ethics.[33] After millenia without a sovereign Jewish state, Jews either have to relate what remained a hypothetical, idealistic, messianic tradition to the messy complexity of military and political reality, or to reject the notion that the tradition can be applied altogether. Ideological choices already enter with the attempt to derive a medieval textual basis for a practical *halakhah* of war. A weighty strand of medieval commentators preferred an idealized Messiah figure who would not even hypothetically be a military man.[34] For Maimonides, by contrast, the military role of a messianic pretender was more than hypothetical. In a letter to the Jews of Provence, he invoked the lack of military training as a cause of the fall of the Temple, implying that it reflected a broader moral malaise which contributed to the Temple's destruction.[35] Nevertheless, his treatment of the subject in 'Kings and Their Wars' is determinedly idealistic about the King, who has personally to follow the most rigorous demands of Torah observance.[36] Whether this image of the King only describes an ideal Messiah – as Michael Walzer has argued[37] – is not wholly clarified in the text, though Maimonides gives an implicit hint that these guidelines could guide Jewish leaders before Messianic times, concluding that in Messianic times the normal rules of war and politics will apply.[38] The question poses itself differently for writers who

[31] Eugene Korn, 'Editor's Introduction to the Shevat 5767 Edition' and 'Conversation: Ethics and Warfare' in *Me'orot* 6:1 (Shevat 5767 / 2006), 4.

[32] Bleich, *Contemporary Halakhic Problems* (New York: Ktav, 1977), Vol. I, 15–16; Noam Zohar, 'Morality and War: A Critique of Bleich's Oracular Halakha' in Daniel H. Frank, ed., *Commandment and Community: New Essays in Jewish Legal and Political Philosophy* (Albany: SUNY Press, 1995), 252.

[33] Stuart A. Cohen, 'The Re-Discovery of Orthodox Jewish Laws Relating to the Military and War (*Hilkhot Tzavah U-Milchamah*) in Contemporary Israel: Trends and Implications' in *Israel Studies* 12:2 (2007), 1–28; Edrei, 'Law, Interpretation, and Ideology', 188–227.

[34] Richard G. Marks, *The Image of Bar Kokhba in Traditional Jewish Literature: False Messiah and National Hero* (University Park PA: Pennslyvania State University Press, 1993), 57–80; George Wilkes, 'Religious War in the Works of Maimonides and the "Maimonideans": An idea and its transit across the medieval Mediterranean' in Sohail Hashmi, ed., *Just Wars, Holy Wars, and Jihads: Christian, Jewish, Muslim Encounters and Exchanges*, forthcoming.

[35] Maimonides, 'Letter on Astrology', trans. Ralph Lerner, in Isadore Twersky, ed., *A Maimonides Reader* (New York: Behrman House, 1972), 465.

[36] *Mishneh Torah*, 'Kings and Their Wars', chapters 1–3.

[37] Michael Walzer, *Law, Politics and Morality in Judaism* (Princeton: Princeton University Press, 2006), 160.

[38] *Mishneh Torah*, 'Kings and Their Wars', 12:1.

juxtapose the modern development of a Jewish polity with centuries of exile. The argument that Jews had no practical experience of military affairs is commonly joined to a critique of historic elements of Jewish tradition deemed to be too influenced by the experience of powerlessness to provide an ethic for the responsible use of force. Progressive writers have identified the influence of a wild Greek militarism on the development of the thought of Maimonides and his modern Zionist successors alike,[39] while National Religious moderates such as Gerald Blidstein have begun to unpick the medieval Islamic ideology which shaped *Kings and Their Wars*,[40] and a range of advocates of a Right-wing hawkish Israeli defence policy have pilloried classic Jewish responses to power as weak-minded assimilationist responses to wider society, whether Roman or Enlightened and European.[41] The reconstruction of the Jewish laws of war is tied to a difficult retrospective historical assessment, and it is easy for anachronism to creep into the generalisations that are so often invoked. No doubt, for instance, Maimonides' approach can be depicted as ideological,[42] though his texts relating to war also reflect a heavy dose of realism, or pessimism.

Tempting as it is to focus on the remarkable shift from the absence of state, army or security to full armed statehood, none of these by themselves need provide a functioning norm for the use of force. It scarcely need be said that each sector of the Israeli Jewish public, secular, *haredi* and *dati*, is divided over what they perceive to be the basic norms by which the security of a Jewish state should be maintained. With power certainly come new conceptions of what constitutes practical, pragmatic, necessary and realistic. In order to become entrenched in army doctrine, or to be widely accepted in public and political discourse, these notions need not be coherent, nor authentically Jewish, nor far-sighted, grounds on which Israelis have criticized both the broadly-accepted innovations of a 'purity of arms' doctrine and the notion that Israel fights wars because the Jewish people are given 'no choice'.[43] Nor need these new conceptions engage with the frameworks which motivate the more philosophical accounts of what makes justifiable military conduct, and what is cause for shame. In the Roman, Christian and Islamic equivalents of the just war traditions, this philosophical core of the laws of war was perennially honoured by rulers in the breach, and taught by lawyers and philosophers who exercised no military power, nor sought to. To take the most obvious example: Aquinas, who is said to have advised Louis VIII on affairs of state, did not write his account of the just war as a manual for a prince. It is aimed at a far wider audience, encompassing not only those for whom war was a tool of politics but also those who saw war as repugnant.[44]

A great proportion of those who write on Jewish military ethics today are experts not in military affairs, but in philosophical ethics, in political thought and in Jewish thought or *halakhah*. Amongst these scholars, the impact of war on the Jewish people is as evident a

---

[39] See, for example, Dow Marmur, *Beyond Survival: Reflections on the Future of Judaism* (London: Darton, Longman & Todd, 1982).

[40] Gerald Blidstein, 'Holy War in Maimonidean Judaism' in Joel Kraemer, ed., *Perspectives on Maimonides* (Oxford: Oxford University Press, 1991), 211–212, 215.

[41] For example Ruth Wisse, *Jews and Power* (New York: Schocken, 2007).

[42] Blidstein, 'Holy War in Maimonidean Judaism' in Kraemer, ed., *Perspectives on Maimonides*, especially 211.

[43] On the 'purity of arms', see Benjamin Ish-Shalom, ' "Purity of Arms" and Purity of Ethical Judgement' in *Me'orot* 6:1 (Shevat 5767 / 2006), 53–61, and Michael Broyde's response, 62–67. On the 'no choice' doctrine, see Ahron Bregman, *Israel's Wars, 1948–1993* (London: Routledge, 2000).

[44] Thomas Aquinas, *Summa Theologiae*, ii–ii, Q. 40, 'On War'.

motive for the development of a Jewish ethical framework for the use of force as are calculations about the effective use of armed force. This balance can be matched from Biblical and Rabbinic texts. Alongside the commentaries on *Kings and Their Wars*, *halakhic* commentators have drawn on a countervalent textual tradition in which war is presented as a state of affairs governed by cruelty and excess, an anarchy which takes over regardless of the aims, strength and methods of the parties to a conflict. War is a state of uncontrolled instability, of crisis, as Joseph B. Soloveitchik put it.[45] Emmanuel Levinas sees this perspective in a rabbinic observation about the attempt to introduce control in city policing, and applies it to war as the extreme situation in which the urge to translate norm into practice confronts reality.[46] This definition of war as an experience, with domestic parallels, opens the debate to a far wider group without military expertise. The powerless know this experience, perhaps more than those in power. For a figure seeking to revive interest in the Jewish text as a locus for contemporary legal and ethical reflection – a key motivation for Levinas, or for Michael Walzer, for instance – centuries of Diasporic experience provide a distinctive resource for reflection on war. Jews have not had an unbroken tradition of sovereignty, but they have been at the receiving end of wars, judging some well-conceived and others misconceived. In treating warfare as an experience, Jewish political thinkers might hope for at least as wide a range of normative sensitivities from Diasporic Judaism as is to be found in the commentaries of the recognized Christian or Muslim authorities on the subject, generally also working at one remove from the political establishment.

3. Is war a proper subject for a distinctive Jewish law or ethic?

Faced with the difficulties inherent in imposing any kind of law on a chaotic medium such as war, Jewish commentators have offered very different responses to the question: Is war a proper subject for Jewish law and ethical exhortation?

A negative response to this question has long typified a quietist Jewish literature for which war is a 'gentile' pursuit, a perspective drawing on isolationist passages in the major Prophets but commonly identified with the period of exile during the two thousand years following the destruction of the Second Temple in 70 CE. This gentile warfare was neither sanctioned, nor was it classically expected, without a Messianic moment.[47] In the post-1945 literature we are covering here, such expectations have been met with three forms of rebuttal, one typically non-Orthodox, another more prevalent within various Orthodox communities, and a third and fourth typifying both traditionalist and progressive figures with a commitment respectively to ethics or spirituality in public life. Firstly, Jacob Agus, an American Conservative rabbi, condemned the notion of allowing war to occupy a lawless zone as a form of idolatry.[48] Agus agreed that Jews have been distinctively isolated from 'the wars of the nations', and that neither pacifism nor militarism can be said to be a clear imperative of

---

[45] Joseph Soloveitchik, 'Insights', lecture delivered 6 January 1979, http://www.613.org/rav/ravnotes2.html#jan0679

[46] Emmanuel Levinas, 'Essai d'analyse philosophique de la guerre', in Jean Halpérin and Georges Levitte, eds., *La conscience juive face à la guerre: données et débats* (Paris: Presses Universitaires de France, 1976), 11–26.

[47] Walzer, *Law, Politics and Morality in Judaism*, 153, 160–61.

[48] Agus, 'A Jewish View of the Problem of War' in *Dimensions of Peace*, 2–4.

religious faith. On the other hand, the ideals inspired by that religious faith, he claimed, are critical tools for public discussion of the fundamental grounds for working towards international peace.[49]

The second rebuttal is embodied in a classic Orthodox response promoted in the work of Michael Broyde.[50] According to Broyde, the *halakhah* allows for a difference between Jewish responsibilities in making war and peace and those of 'the nations of the world', with the law restricting Jewish more than it does other nations.[51] Sharon Last Stone contrasts this dualistic approach to law with a more universalistic approach, open to the influence of contemporary international law on *halakhah*, for Jews as well as the nations at large.[52] In this third perspective, the notional division between Jewish and non-Jewish war undermines efforts to address the gaps which war and other international challenges open up for the law-maker.[53]

A fourth rebuttal acknowledges that war spins out of control, but finds grounds for an ethical response in the role of the passions and of self-interest in creating conflict. War is, particularly within literature focused on a more spiritually-defined ethics, a spiritual challenge. Where it is viewed as the archetypal challenge to the quest for a disciplined obedience to law and to external ethical limitations, it can also be presented as the archetypal situation in which law and ethical restraint are necessary. Thus, Deuteronomy 20 is followed by the 'beautiful captive' passage (Deuteronomy 21: 10–14), laying down rules to control the bestial urges of the soldier when confronted with a vulnerable female in the heat of battle. Michael Walzer has argued that this text is definitive of a historic 'just war' tradition of recognising the rights of the individual in wartime.[54] The Progressive rabbi Edward Feinstein used the text to argue that the chaos of war is exactly where ethical restraint must be asserted – that the 'beautiful captive' text presents an archetypal situation of spiritual contest for the Jewish ethicist.[55]

These competing positions suggest a distinctive ethical motivation for imposing limitations on war, and the corollary to these positions is the assumption that a distinctive ethical contribution to international politics can be effective. Others, at the other end of the spectrum, and often in the context of *halakhic* debate rather than as part of a broader ethical exhortation, argue that the nature of war makes it uncontrollable, wild, and uncivilised. In Saadia Gaon's *Emunot ve-Deot*, war is touched upon only as a catastrophe or a divine visitation, not as an ethical challenge,[56] and this is true of many medieval commentaries. But in those *halakhic* texts where a doctrine of self-defence is established, the lawlessness of war has ethical

---

[49] Agus, 'A Jewish View of the Problem of War' in *Dimensions of Peace*, 2–4.

[50] For example Broyde, 'Just Wars, Just Battles and Just Conduct in Jewish Law' in Schiffman and Wolowelsky, eds., *War and Peace in the Jewish Tradition*, 1–44; and 'Only the Good Die Young?' in *Me'orot* 6:1 (Shevat 5767 / 2006), 62–67.

[51] Broyde, 'Just Wars, Just Battles and Just Conduct in Jewish Law' in Schiffman and Wolowelsky, eds., *War and Peace in the Jewish Tradition*, 9–17.

[52] Sharon Last Stone, 'The Jewish Law of War: The Turn to International Law and Ethics' in Sohail Hashmi, ed., *Just Wars, Holy Wars, and Jihads: Christian, Jewish, Muslim Encounters and Exchanges*, forthcoming.

[53] Stone, 'The Jewish Law of War' in Hashmi, ed., *Just Wars, Holy Wars, and Jihads*.

[54] Michael Walzer, *Just and Unjust Wars* (New York: Basic Books, 1977), 134–135.

[55] Edward Feinstein, cited in Wilkes, 'Judaism and Justice in War' in Robinson, ed., *Just War in Comparative Perspective*, 14.

[56] Saadia Gaon, *The Book of Beliefs and Opinions*, trans. Samuel Rosenblatt (New Haven: Yale University Press, 1948).

implications. One Modern Orthodox and *haredi* response is to assert that the uncivilizable chaos of war removes all moral limits on the use of force once a war is launched. Restraint, according to this view, belongs to the period before battle is commenced, and then it becomes immoral. Thus, Menachem Mendel Schneerson, the last Lubavitcher Rebbe, consistently rejected any projected ceasefire in Lebanon in 1982, basing his rejection in terms of the continuing threat that the enemy posed, and by reference to a series of biblical verses which he believed assure 'complete victory' for those who trust in the Lord.[57]

The doctrinal opposition to an apparently excessive restraint is not necessarily tantamount to a call for totally unrestrained violence. It may be, however. If war is essentially wild and chaotic, then focused, purposive, necessary violence becomes very difficult to measure. Broyde adopts a position acknowledging both the virtually lawless nature of war, and the duty to impose law on that chaos. In Broyde's view, war demands a readiness to suspend normal *halakhic* limitations, if necessary by virtue of a *hora'at sha'ah*, temporarily declaring a law to be inapplicable.[58] While this responds to the ungovernable nature of war, Broyde insists that a normative response is appropriate to and demanded by the state of war. War does not make law irrelevant, because without legal sanction killing for a religious Jew is murder. The law in wartime, however, has to be different in order to preserve the possibility of a normative order.

The significance of the range of normative options canvassed in the literature can be further clarified through the decisions these normative options imply. To make judgements in response to the chaotic nature of war, a range of commentators rely upon experts, and which experts they favour speaks volumes about the normative framework into which war is placed. In 1967, Joseph Soloveitchik urged rabbis to defer to military experts when faced with requests for guidance on questions of war and peace, though earlier in his career he took a more ebullient *halakhic* line in insisting both that military achievements were in the hands of God and that rabbis ought not to be excluded from the public realm.[59] According to Menachem Mendel Schneerson, the judgements of the military were of definitive importance because of their expertise, though in his view these judgements became 'the *halakhah*', rather than restricting the scope for *halakhic* guidance.[60] Amongst more determinedly *haredi* commentators, this respect for military experts is commonly balanced by an affirmative view that the great sages of the day, the *gedolei hador*, have a special purchase on both the true *halakhic* answer and the prospect of victory or defeat, which lie in God's hands.[61] The rabbis may, alternatively, be credited with a superior ethical perspective. Thus, according to one of the most respected right wing Modern Orthodox rabbis, the late Chaim Zimmerman, military men cannot be trusted with decisions about lives at stake in wartime because of the crude statistical approach they have in calculating the effect of military actions on lives (here

---

[57] 'Fulfillment of Mission', translation from addresses given in 1982, published in Menachem Mendel Schneerson, *Peace For The Galilee: Sichos In English, Excerpts of Sichos delivered by The Lubavitcher Rebbe, Rabbi Menachem M. Schneerson*, Vol. 14 Sivan-Elul 5742/1982 (Brooklyn NY: Committee for Sichos in English, 5744/1984).

[58] Broyde, 'Only the Good Die Young?' in *Me'orot* 6:1 (Shevat 5767 / 2006), 46.

[59] On Soloveitchik's much-noted Teshuvah shiur at the 92nd Street YMCA, September 1967, see for example Haskel Lookstein, 'A Mission Fulfilled' in *Jewish Action* (Spring 2003/5763), 3. On Soloveitchik's earlier views, see Shalom Carmy, ' "The Heart Pained by the Pain of the People": Rabbinic Leadership in Two Discussions by R. Joseph B. Soloveitchik' in *Torah u-Madda* (13/2005), 1–14, here 3.

[60] 'Fulfillment of Mission' in Schneerson, *Peace For The Galilee*.

[61] For a critical reflection, see Lawrence Kaplan, '*Daas Torah*: A Modern Conception of Rabbinic Authority' in Moshe Sokol, ed., *Rabbinic Authority and Personal Autonomy* (Northvale NJ: Jason Aronson, 1992), 1–60.

he is referring to Jewish lives, specifically). The rabbis, by contrast, are devoted to a much stricter level of commitment to individual life.[62]

Against these positions, a growing body of more liberal, communitarian commentators – among whom Michael Walzer is both representative and influential – promote a distinctive Jewish political engagement with international political problems faced not by Jews alone but by the nations of the world as a whole, in which the expertise deemed most crucial to the making of war and peace is political and more broadly philosophical. The role of the political expert is not only to provide a check on military and executive, though in this vein of literature, increasing stress has been laid on the role of a democratic assembly in war-making powers.[63] Recognising the moral and political nature of war, political experts are envisaged here to guide public debate towards effective long-term commitments, as much from outside Parliament as from within it. What is effective or 'practical' in this communitarian perspective is not primarily defined by short-term calculation, nor does it propose long-term certainties where the unpredictability of war prevents this. If they are vulnerable to charges of political or military impracticality, Jewish communitarians nevertheless insist that a distinctive religious Jewish contribution to political and military affairs must comprise a long-term commitment to a collective ethical or human dimension or it will either cease to be Jewish or it will cease to be politically relevant. Moral commitment, to the 'purity of arms' or to the sanctity of the lives of individual soldiers, makes a core feature of this communitarian politics, and is in this view worth the risk it entails to national security and the lives of individual soldiers.[64]

Conclusion

Above, we have seen the practical limitations to normative Jewish teaching on the making of war and peace. The burgeoning body of literature on Jewish approaches to war asserts that, because of this, there is a need for renewed debate over Jewish approaches to war, and in spite of this, Jewish norms must apply to war.

The lack of practical experience of sovereignty and war-making in previous centuries does not discourage some commentators from judging Jewish tradition to be more 'realistic' about war than its Christian counterparts – a generalisation promoted by Michael Broyde,[65] as it had been in the 1920s by Franz Rosenzweig.[66] Similarly, Michael Walzer and fellow communitarians see Jewish tradition as a distinctive and particularly valuable source of

---

[62] Chaim Zimmerman, 'The Prohibition of Abandoning Land in Eretz-Yisrael', *Ariel Center for Policy Research Policy Paper* 158 (March 2005).

[63] See, notably, Noam Zohar, 'Morality and War: A Critique of Bleich's Oracular Halakha' in Daniel H. Frank, ed., *Commandment and Community: New Essays in Jewish Legal and Political Philosophy* (Albany: SUNY Press, 1995), 245–258; Walzer, ed., *Law, Politics and Morality in Judaism*. For a broader background to the project, see, for example, Daniel Elazar, ed., *Morality and Power: Contemporary Jewish Views* (Lanham MD: University Press of America / Jerusalem, Jerusalem Center for Public Affairs, 1989), and Michael Walzer, Menahem Lorberbaum and Noam Zohar, eds., *The Jewish Political Tradition*, Vol. 1 (Authority, New Haven CT: Yale University Press, 2000).

[64] Benjamin Ish-Shalom insists on a close parallel to this in his defence of 'the purity of arms', in ' "Purity of Arms" and Purity of Ethical Judgement' in *Me'orot* 6:1 (Shevat 5767 / 2006), 53–61.

[65] Broyde, 'Fighting the War and the Peace' in Burns, ed., *War and Its Discontents*, 1–30, here 24n.29.

[66] Franz Rosenzweig, *The Star of Redemption*, translated from the 2nd ed. of 1930 by William W. Hallo (New York: Holt, Rinehart and Winston, 1971), 331.

reflection on war because Jewish tradition highlights the human context in which war is fought.[67]

A vibrant sense of the need for normative teaching on war therefore coexists in both Orthodox and non-Orthodox Jewish literature with an equally vigorous dispute over the ambivalent nature of that normative body of law. The military situation of both the State of Israel and the United States of America has persuaded many that the recovery or development of a distinctively Jewish approach to the laws of war is a matter of urgency, whether this distinctive approach promotes or counters an effective resort to warfare. In much of this literature, the extent of the divergence of opinion within the Jewish community is the subject of extended deliberation. The limits or ambiguities of the textual resources available are examined alongside the argumentative and intellectual strategies by which these limits are overcome by partisans of the competing positions in the debate. Clearly, many protagonists in the debate find the diversity of opinion problematic. For that reason, it would be unwise to imagine this new genre of Jewish 'war and peace' ethics as evidence of an embracing pluralism. Neither are many of the essays covered here evidence of raw, unnuanced polemic. In their combination of commitment and ambivalence, they provide an excellent resource for the student of contemporary Jewish normative strategies when faced with little consensus in respect to the authorities most appropriate for the task, and less with regard to the nature of the practicalities involved. The resultant diversity feeds on the sense that for Judaism to be Judaism it must present normative responses to the dilemmas faced in such an important aspect of Jewish life.

BIBLIOGRAPHY

Biale, David, *Power and Powerlessness in Jewish History* (New York: Schocken Books, 1986).

Bleich, J. David, *Contemporary Halakhic Problems* (New York: Ktav/Yeshiva University Press, 1977–1989), Vols I–III.

Bregman, Ahron, *Israel's Wars, 1948–1993* (London: Routledge, 2000).

Brekke, Torkel, ed., *The Ethics of War in Asian Civilizations: A Comparative Perspective* (Abingdon/New York: Routledge, 2006).

Broyde, Michael, 'Only the Good Die Young?', *Me'orot* 6:1 (Shevat 5767/2006) 62–67.

Carmy, Shalom, ' "The Heart Pained by the Pain of the People": Rabbinic Leadership in Two Discussions by R. Joseph B. Soloveitchik', *Torah u-Madda* (13/2005), 1–14

Central Conference of American Rabbis, 'Preventive War', CCAR Responsa (5762.8), http://data.ccarnet.org/cgi-bin/respdisp.pl?file=8&year=5762.

Cohen, Stuart A., 'The Re-Discovery of Orthodox Jewish Laws Relating to the Military and War (*Hilkhot Tzavah U-Milchamah*) in Contemporary Israel: Trends and Implications,' *Israel Studies* 12:2 (2007), 1–28.

Dimensions of Peace: A Jewish Confrontation. Report of a Conference on the Relevance of Jewish Tradition to the Problems of a Nuclear Age (New York: Dimensions of Peace, 1963).

---

[67] Walzer, *Just and Unjust Wars*, notably 168. A comparable teaching explored by one of the leading communitarians within the Jewish renewal movement, Arthur Waskow, may be found in 'Gentle Hearts and Coronets', *Jerusalem Report* (4 September 2006), originally written as 'Soldiers, Kings, and the "Gentle Heart": Torah & Today' (2002), available at http://www.shalomctr.org/node/1171

Edrei, Arye, 'Divine Spirit and Physical Power: Rabbi Shlomo Goren and the Military Ethic of the Israel Defense Forces', *Theoretical Inquiries in Law* 7/1 (January 2006), 255–297.

Edrei, Arye, 'Law, Interpretation, and Ideology: The Renewal of the Jewish Laws of War in the State of Israel,' *Cardozo Law Review* 28:1 (2006), 188–227.

Elazar, Daniel, ed., *Morality and Power: Contemporary Jewish Views* (Lanham MD: University Press of America / Jerusalem, Jerusalem Center for Public Affairs, 1989).

Frank, Daniel H., ed., *Commandment and Community: New Essays in Jewish Legal and Political Philosophy* (Albany: SUNY Press, 1995).

Halpérin, Jean, and Georges Levitte, eds., *La conscience juive face à la guerre: données et débats* (Paris: Presses Universitaires de France, 1976).

Hashmi, Sohail, ed., *Just Wars, Holy Wars, and Jihads: Christian, Jewish, Muslim Encounters and Exchanges*, forthcoming.

Hogan, Linda, and Dylan Lehrke, eds., *Religion And The Politics Of Peace And Conflict* (Eugene OR: Wipf & Stock, 2009).

Ish-Shalom, Benjamin, ' "Purity of Arms" and Purity of Ethical Judgement', *Me'orot* (6:1) Shevat 5767 (2006), 53–61.

Kagan, Israel Meir (the Chafetz Chaim), *Mahane Yisrael* (New York: Shulsinger Brothers, 1943).

Kelley, Nicole, 'The Cosmopolitan Expression of Josephus's Prophetic Perspective in the *Jewish War*', *Harvard Theological Review* 97:3 (2004), 257–74.

Kellner, Menachem, ed., *Contemporary Jewish Ethics* (New York: Sanhedrin Press, 1978).

Korn, Eugene, 'Editor's Introduction to the Shevat 5767 Edition', *Me'orot* 6:1 (Shevat 5767 / 2006), 4.

Kraemer, Joel, ed., *Perspectives on Maimonides* (Oxford: Oxford University Press, 1991).

Levey, Geoffrey B., 'Judaism and the Obligation to Die for the State', *AJS Review* 12:2 (Autumn 1987), 175–203.

Lookstein, Haskel, 'A Mission Fulfilled', *Jewish Action* (Spring 2003/5763), 3–6.

Marks, Richard G., *The Image of Bar Kokhba in Traditional Jewish Literature: False Messiah and National Hero* (University Park PA: Pennslyvania State University Press, 1993).

Marmur, Dow, *Beyond Survival: Reflections on the Future of Judaism* (London: Darton, Longman & Todd, 1982).

Nahari, Chaniel, 'The Development of Halakhic Literature for Soldiers from 1880–1975,' Bar-Ilan University, MA thesis, 2003.

Patout Burns, J., ed., *War and Its Discontents: Pacifism and Quietism in the Abrahamic Religions* (Washington D.C.: Georgetown University Press, 1996).

Polner, Murray, and Naomi Goodman, eds., *The Challenge of Shalom: The Jewish Tradition of Peace and Justice* (Philadelphia: New Society Publishers, 1994).

Polner, Murray, and Stefan Merken, *Peace, Justice and Jews: Reclaiming Our Tradition* (New York: Bunim & Bannigan, 2007).

Robinson, Paul A., ed., *Just War in Comparative Perspective* (Aldershot: Ashgate Press, 2003).

Rodin, David, and Richard Sorabji, eds., *The Ethics of War: Shared Problems in Different Traditions* (Aldershot: Ashgate Press, 2006).

Rosenzweig, Franz, *The Star of Redemption*, translated from the 2nd ed. of 1930 by William W. Hallo (New York: Holt, Rinehart and Winston, 1971).

Schiffman, Lawrence, and Joel B. Wolowelsky, eds., *War and Peace in the Jewish Tradition* (New York: Yeshiva University Press, 2007).

Schneerson, Menachem Mendel, *Peace For The Galilee: Sichos In English, Excerpts of Sichos delivered by The Lubavitcher Rebbe, Rabbi Menachem M. Schneerson*, Vol. 14 Sivan-Elul 5742/1982 (Brooklyn NY: Committee for Sichos in English, 5744/1984).

Sokol, Moshe, ed., *Rabbinic Authority and Personal Autonomy* (Northvale NJ: Jason Aronson, 1992).

Soloveitchik, Joseph, 'Insights', lecture delivered 6 January 1979, http://www.613.org/rav/ravnotes2.html#jan0679.

Twersky, Isadore, ed., *A Maimonides Reader* (New York: Behrman House, 1972).

Walzer, Michael, *Just and Unjust Wars: a moral argument with historical illustrations* 1st ed. (New York: Basic Books, 1977).

Walzer, Michael, Menahem Lorberbaum, & Noam Zohar, eds., *The Jewish Political Tradition*, Vol. 1 (Authority, New Haven CT: Yale University Press, 2000).

Walzer, Michael, ed., *Law, Politics and Morality in Judaism* (Princeton: Princeton University Press, 2006).

Waskow, Arthur, may be found in 'Gentle Hearts and Coronets', *Jerusalem Report* (4 September 2006), originally written as 'Soldiers, Kings, and the "Gentle Heart": Torah & Today' (2002), available at http://www.shalomctr.org/node/1171.

Wellman, James K., ed., *Belief and Bloodshed: Religion and Violence across Time and Tradition* (Lanham MD: Rowman & Littlefield, 2007).

Wisse, Ruth, *Jews and Power* (New York: Schocken, 2007).

Zimmerman, Chaim, 'The Prohibition of Abandoning Land in Eretz-Yisrael', *Ariel Center for Policy Research Policy Paper* 158 (March 2005).

WHOSE MUSIC? OWNERSHIP AND IDENTITY IN JEWISH MUSIC

Ruth Rosenfelder*

The specific effect of music on the human mind has been explored by clinical psychiatrist Oliver Sacks, and responses to music have been examined by social philosophers such as Theodor Adorno. Their findings reveal the importance of music both on a personal level and as a social indicator. It would therefore seem axiomatic that music is a defining constituent in the taxonomy of any culture, whilst religious music, with integrated elements of spirituality, is particularly powerful in emoting direct and profound response and recognition. The biblical text indicates the centrality of music in all aspects of daily as well as religious life, although evidence of musical notation or of the sounds of chant or melody, sacred or other, has yet to come to light. The post-Biblical addition of a 2000 year Diaspora in which Jewish communities were established throughout the world, implies an additional absorption of the musics of a variety of host societies. Nevertheless, the tropes of Ashkenazi liturgy as well as genres such as Klezmer and the folk music of both Ashkenazi and Sephardi European Jewry are generally regarded as identifiably 'Jewish'. This paper explores attitudes to musical appropriation and intercultural exchange in religious, para-liturgical and domestic music, and also considers notions of 'sacred' and 'profane' in a Jewish musical context, with particular emphasis on Hasidic religious ideology and the Sephardi women's folk tradition.

Whose Music? Ownership and Identity in Jewish Music

The effect of music is not merely powerful but arguably evokes the most visceral of human responses. Social philosophers such as Theodor Adorno explore reactions to music in theoretical terms whilst the neurologist Oliver Sacks describes physical manifestations caused by the effects of music, both known and unknown, on his patients.[1] In the case of music that is familiar, Sacks states that the melody, 'acts as a Proustian mnemonic ... giving the patient access to moods and memories ... that had seemingly been completely lost'.

In many religions, music, in the form of hymns, anthems, incantations or chants, is a vital element in attempting to achieve spirituality. In the case of Judaism, probably the most universally recognized Jewish liturgical melody is that sung to the prayer *Kol Nidrei* at the start of the most solemn day in the Jewish calendar, *Yom Kippur*. It is one of approximately ten melodies that are sung during the *Yomim Noroyim* (Heb. 'High Holydays' using traditional Ashkenazi pronunciation); the origins of these melodies are unknown but are believed to be so ancient as to warrant the title *Mi Sinai* (Heb. 'From Sinai').[2] Whilst regarded as belonging

* Visiting Lecturer in Jewish Music Studies, City University, London. Email: r.rosenfelder@city.ac.uk

[1] Theodor Adornon, *Beethoven: The Philosophy of Music* (Palo Alto: Stanford University Press, 1997). Oliver Sacks, *Musicophilia* (New York: Alfred A. Knopf, 2007), 344–347.

[2] See 'Mi Sinai Niggunim', *Encyclopedia Judaica*, (Israel: CD Rom Edition, Israel: Judaica Multimedia Ltd., 1997).

within the relative confines of the *Ashkenazi* tradition, general awareness of the *Kol Nidrei* [3] melody has extended well beyond a specific Jewish group or even the context of Sacred Service to become a Jewish melodic marker for Jew and non-Jew alike.[4] Thus, this traditional *Ashkenazi* melody may be described as having travelled from the Synagogue into the general musical soundscape whilst maintaining a Jewish identity.

In the context of Sacred Service, music is fundamental to Judaism. With few exceptions, prayers are either chanted or sung, with certain melodies or modes associated with particular festivals, Sabbath or week-day prayers and Torah readings as well as para-liturgical songs and hymns that are sung in the home to celebrate life and annual cycles. However, as a result of the 2000 year Jewish Diaspora, the notion of an essentially, definable 'Jewish' melody is, as demonstrated by the *Kol Nidrei* paradigm, confused by a complex host of musical traditions that now obtain, when setting texts that are often common to all Jewish communities. Thus, implicit differences between, for example, Yemenite and Polish melodies for settings of identical liturgy or Biblical text would indicate inevitable external musical influences.

The Bible, Judaism's primary source, provides many references to music and its practice, but there is as yet no evidence to indicate any melodic structures and surprisingly, given the importance of written documentation demonstrated by Biblical text, there remains a continued absence of any indication of written musical notation.[5] This lack of information encourages many forms of speculation as to instrumentation and general performance practice, particularly in Temple service, since the many references and Talmudic discussions on Temple music indicate its importance.[6] Additionally, there remains a generally held belief that until the actual Temple melodies can be confirmed, all melody, non-sacred as well as religious, must be considered as possibly deriving from Temple sources and should therefore not be regarded as unacceptable.[7]

Hasidism and Music

Acknowledgement of the validity of all melody is further endorsed within Hasidic philosophy, which regards the sacred and profane as inextricably bound together.[8] Thus, a holistic vision

---

[3] *Kol Nidrei* (Aramaic. lit 'All Vows') is the prayer which heralds *Yom Kippur* (Heb. 'Day of Atonement'), the holiest day in the Jewish calendar.

[4] Arguably the most notable example of the *Kol Nidre* melody as thematic material in Western Art music for a non-Jewish composer is *Kol Nidre*, Op.47 for Cello and Orchestra, by Max Bruch (1838–1920). Composed in Liverpool in 1880, in response to a commission from the Liverpool Jewish community, it was first published in Berlin in 1881 and continues to enjoy general popularity in the concert hall and the recording studio.

[5] The discovery, during the middle of the twentieth century, of Mesopotamian cuneiform tablets indicating instrumental tunings and probable musical systems offers encouragement that recorded Ancient Hebrew musical notational system may also be discovered. See particularly the works of Anne Kilmer, Emeritus Professor of Assyriology, University of California at Berkeley, for example 'The Discovery of an Ancient Theory of Mesopotamian Music', *Proceedings of the American Philosophical Society*, 1971, and Joachim Braun, Emeritus Professor of Music, Bar-Ilan University, an example being, J. Braun, *Music in Ancient Israel/Palestine: Archeological, Written and Comparative Sources* (Grand Rapids, Michigan: Eerdmans Publications, 2002).

[6] See, for example, Babelonian Talmud, tractate *Sukkah* 50a, 50b and 51a

[7] Expressed by the scholar and teacher, Rabbi S. Sperber, personal communication with this author in 1961 (exact date unknown) who held the post of the Jewish Agency's Director at the Department for Torah and Education and Culture in London.

[8] For general discussion of Hasidic principles see 'Hasidism', *Encyclopedia Judaica* (1997).

for physical and spiritual well-being. It is therefore totally acceptable to adopt a street or folk song and exalt it by adapting it to the glory of God. There are stories of Hasidic *Rebbes* hearing shepherds in the countryside or organ-grinders in the town singing an attractive song. Typically, the *Rebbe* would ask the singer to teach him the song, sometimes in exchange for a sum of money. As soon as the *Rebbe* had learnt it, the organ grinder or shepherd would forget the melody. Association with the *Rebbe* would then elevate the melody from the mundane to the spiritual. In an brief summary of Hasidic music, writer and musician Velvel Pasternak describes the criticism made by music scholars and opponents of Hasidism that Hasidic music includes what he characterises as 'foreign elements'.[9] He adds, however, that:

> the strains of shepherd melodies ... in no way harmed the sanctity of the melody, for the essence of a *nigun* (Hasidic melody) is the sound, and if the sound is derived from an impure source, there is a duty to elevate, purify and sanctify it until it is worthy of the responsibility for which it was created.[10]

In Hasidic philosophy, non-texted melody is regarded as superior to texted song, as confirmed by Rabbi Shneur Zalman, the first Lubavitcher Rebbe, when he acknowledged, 'The tongue is the pen of the heart, but melody is the pen of the soul'.[11] Untexted music is regarded as a direct conduit between God and Man without the intervention and therefore distraction of the human word. Thus, the frequent occurrence of vocables such as *'Ya bi bom'* or *'Oy yoy yoy'* in place of text in Hasidic song allows the singer to concentrate on melody alone when attempting contemplation to achieve a desired state of ecstasy in prayer.

In pre-World War II Eastern Europe, it appears that adoption of local musical idioms as part of a particular Hasidic group's tradition was not unusual. An example may be found in the compositions by twenty-first century Satmar composers in the traditional style of Satmar *nigun*. Four new melodies are created annually for the *Yomim Neroyim*; these are sung wordlessly but each is associated with a specific High Holyday prayer. The style of the compositions imitates that of the 1930s melodies of Berish Wishower, the Satmarer *Rebbe*'s official composer; each year one is in the style of the folk or popular dance idioms that existed in Austria, Germany, Switzerland and Bohemia, such as the polka or the three-beat *Ländler*, which is thought to be the precursor of the waltz. In an unusual addition of a written liner note to the melodies composed in 2002, the anonymous author describes, in Yiddish, the new compositions as directly deriving from the Wischower Satmar tradition but with no reference to possible melodic origins.[12] Nevertheless, there is an implied presumption that within the canon of Hasidic *nigun* there exists recognizably 'Satmar' melodies, albeit unrecorded on paper.

---

[9] Eli Lipsker and Velvel Pasternak, *Chabad Melodies: Songs of the Lubavitcher Chassidim* (Baltimore: Tara Publications, 1997), 8.

[10] Ibid.

[11] Author unknown, quoted in the notes accompanying cassette recording of Lubavitch *nigunim*, *The Rebbe's Nigunim* (New York: Y&M Music Productions, 1995), 1. For discussion on wordless *nigun*, including particular references to Lubavitch philosophy, see Chemjo Vinaver, *Anthology of Hassidic Music* (Jerusalem: Hebrew University of Jerusalem, 1985), 220–223.

[12] *Nigunei Satmar*, CDD #103 (no further attribution). Two examples of melodies which include Austro-Hungarian folk elements appear on the audio-cassette; one of the melodies is by Wischower. Chemjo Vinaver describes the general Hasidic response to written as opposed to oral transmission of knowledge as 'blasphemy'. Vinaver, *Anthology of Hassidic Music*, 18. Whilst this understanding may be regarded as rather extreme, written sleeve notes appear very rarely to accompany audio-recordings of Satmar *nigunim*.

By contrast, the Lubavitch tradition of recorded scholarship as well the group's history of interaction with peoples outside its own community identifies it as *sui generis* within the Hasidic community. The Lubavitch approach includes acknowledgement of the source of some of its melodies, an example of which is the meditative, wordless *nigun* known as *Shamil's nigun*. Shamil, a nineteenth century Muslim anti-Russian resistance leader based in the Caucuses, was imprisoned by the Russians. Whilst there, he sang a plaintive melody which could be heard from outside his cell and which was subsequently absorbed into the Lubavitch canon of *nigun*.[13] Parallels are drawn between the song representing Shamil's desire for freedom which, as a Lubavitch *nigun*, becomes an expression of the soul's wish to escape the bonds of the human body and return to the freedom of spiritual oneness with God. Now widely known amongst members of Lubavitch, *Shamil's Nigun* was taught by the seventh and most recent Lubavitcher Rebbe, Rabbi Menachem-Mendel Schneerson, known to his followers as the *Rebbe*, in 1958 as part of a drive to reintroduce forgotten Lubavitch melodies and build up a canon of Lubavitch *nigunim*.[14] A two-volume collection of 347 melodies includes words and music, written in five-line Western stave notation, and includes explanatory notes to some of the *nigunim* (pl.).[15]

Texted *nigunim* are generally in Hebrew, often taken from liturgical or Biblical sources, replacing the original lyrics if the melody derives from a folk-song. However, a further example of a Lubavitch exception to Hasidic norms is the *nigun, Essen Est Zich*.[16] The words of the song are in Yiddish, East European Jewry's vernacular, which is unusual for a *nigun*, particularly one of this meditative character. Regarded as a melody to aid concentration in prayer, it is thought to derive from a Russian drinking song, a notion born out by textual references to eating and drinking, '*Essen est zich trinken trinkt zich vos zol men ton az es davent zich nit essen est zich shlofn shloft zich vos zol men ton az es davent zich nit*' (Yidd. 'Eating is simple, drinking is simple, what's to be done if one can't pray; eating is easy, sleeping is easy, what's do be done if one can't pray'). For the Lubavitch member with a problem concerned with prayer, the advice is to substitute prayers for the text in this slow meditative melody with its mantra-like chant. However, a change of tempo transforms the *nigun* from contemplation to rhythmic joy, particularly when it is sung in company at a meal or celebration.

A particularly interesting melody that the *Rebbe* revived is one that sets the words taken from the liturgy, sung in Synagogue on Sabbaths and festivals, '*Ho'aderes veho'emunah*' (Heb. 'Power and trustworthiness') juxtaposed with Hasidic 'lai la lai'. In 1973, The *Rebbe*, who had studied in France, presented the melody that was then no longer in use, explaining that the first *Lubavitcher Rebbe*, Rabbi Shneur Zalman of Lyadi, heard it sung by Napoleon's army during its Russian campaign and had asked for it to be sung to him. It is in fact the melody to the *Marseilles*, which by adoption, the first *Lubavitcher Rebbe* transformed into a holy melody, a typical example of cultural and spiritual transformation. In 1992, the *Rebbe* returned to the subject of the melody and a recent further transformation it had undergone. He began by reminding his followers that they had begun to sing the melody of the French national anthem to religious text in 1973. He continued,

---

[13] The melody can be heard on cassette audio-recording, *The Rebbe's Nigunim* (1995).

[14] The *Rebbe* died in 1994 without a successor.

[15] Samuel Zalmanoff, *Sefer Hanigunim* (Brooklyn: Nichoach, no date).

[16] For the *nigun* see Samuel Zalmanoff, *Sefer Hanigunim*, 1:109, 97. Transliterated Yiddish text, traditionally written in Hebrew characters, is taken from Lipsker, *Chabad Melodies*, 45.

A short while later... an incredible phenomenon transpired: the French people, in compliance with their Prime Minister's suggestion, modified the melody and softened its rhythm... What had induced this spontaneous change? When the *nigun* had been transformed into holiness, the heavenly angel and spiritual source of the nation of France perceived the transformation. This triggered the sudden reaction to alter the song, resulting from the inherent realisation of their spiritual source, that this anthem which had previously embodied the French nation is no longer exclusively theirs. It now belongs to the domain of holiness.[17]

The *Rebbe* acknowledges not merely the origins of the Marseilles, but that it remains as the country's anthem. It is not therefore a case of total religious transformation as in the examples of the shepherd forgetting the melody once it has been elevated to spiritual levels. What the *Rebbe* declares is that by adopting the melody, presumably without the awareness of any French official or politician, Lubavitch has prompted a softening in the French national psyche. The melody is therefore no longer the sole property of the French; because of Lubavitch's intervention, it has attained a spiritual universality as well as a shared identity. The notion of melody as an essentialist nationalist marker is thus denied in favour of melody as a supernatural phenomenon that can be adapted through spiritual intervention.

The Tradition of Sephardi *Women's Music*

The *Rebbe*'s revival of Lubavitch *nigunim* was part of a programme to regenerate the group's endangered traditions in the wake of World War II and its relocation to the United States. Acts to preserve threatened religious and cultural practices run like a *leitmotif* throughout Jewish history, such as the additional readings to those of the Torah instigated by Ezra as a result of the Babylonian exile, or Y*ehudah Ha' Nasi*'s redaction of the *Mishnah* and the subsequent recording of dialectics in the *Talmud*. In the context of this paper, the tradition of women's folksong, particularly that of Sephardi women, who originated from the Iberian Peninsula, is of particular relevance. The demonstration of intercultural exchange, or indeed its absence, through music, is advanced by the musicologist Abraham Zvi Idelsohn. He argues that confinement to the ghetto endured by generations of Ashkenazi communities caused them to turn inward, essentially to the music of the Synagogue, for their folk and domestic melodies.[18] Ashkenazi liturgical melodies and motifs, although essentially an orally sustained tradition, developed into recognizable *Shtayger* (Yidd. lit. 'Scales'), modes that evolved from motifs and melodies associated with particular prayers. Although Ashkenazi women scarcely attended synagogue, they developed their own body of Yiddish written supplications, known as *t'khines*, as well as Yiddish translations of epic poems and ballads which they shaped to relate to particularly Jewish concerns. Ashkenazi women's literacy, at a time when few men and fewer women were generally capable of reading, is demonstrated by the particular Hebrew characters they used for their Yiddish writings. The cursive script they adopted became so recognizable that it came to be known as *Wayber-taytsch* (Yidd.

---

[17] Taken from notes accompanying *The Rebbe's Nigunim*, 18. An official at the Ministry of Culture in Paris confirmed that, on taking office in 1974, President Giscard d'Estang initiated a change of orchestration to soften the composition's martial elements. The new version was first played at his inauguration ceremony at the Arc de Triomphe and was subsequently adopted. The official added, however, that she thought the trend was towards reverting to the original instrumentation. Personal telephone communication (3 May 2000).

[18] Abraham Z. Idelsohn, *Jewish Music: Its Historical Development*, (New York: Schocken Books, 1967), 379.

'women's version').[19] It may be assumed that the verses were either sung or chanted to existing melodies, particularly since some *t'khines* have indications in their sub-headings naming the tune of a song to which the supplication should be sung. Nevertheless, there would seem to be little melodic evidence that may safely be solely associated with the Ashkenazi women's body of songs. What is certain however is that the texts that Ashkenazi women sang were in Yiddish and would have therefore been translated and adapted from any non-Ashkenazi source such as the *minnesinger* or other street singers.

By contrast, the songs of their Sephardi counterparts would appear to have been sung exactly as they heard them in the streets of medieval Spain and have remained intact until the present. This occurred, in spite of, or perhaps because of, their expulsion from Spain and Portugal, possibly demonstrating their need to retain a defined identity as a doubly displace Diaspora minority group. Following their expulsion in the last decade of the 15th century, Sephardi communities were established throughout Europe, into Greece, the Balkans, and North Africa, side by side with existing Jewish communities. The Sephardim took with them a written corpus of medieval poetry, *piyyutim* (Heb. 'liturgical poems') written mainly in Hebrew or Aramaic, many of which would eventually become incorporated into Synagogue liturgy and the para-liturgical hymns sung in the homes within both Ashkenazi as well Sephardi tradition. Sephardi folk and domestic music was, by contrast passed down orally and stemmed from the street songs that would have been sung by the *joglares* and *segrels*, the Iberian equivalent of the German *minnesinger* or the French *troubadours* and *jongleurs*. The language of Sephardi songs contrasts with Europe's Ashkenazi communities whose isolation within Russia and Poland is demonstrated in the development of a specifically Jewish argot, *Yiddish*, based on German but with much additional Hebrew. Whilst German was the second language of the educated classes in those countries under Austro-Hungarian rule, it was not generally Eastern Europe vernacular, and certainly not in countries within the Russian Empire where French was generally the second language.

In marked difference, Sephardi cultural integration is indicated by the fact that Sephardi Judeo-Spanish vernacular, *Judezmo*, referred to as Ladino, was essentially Castillian Spanish to which occasional Hebrew or Aramaic words were added.[20] The songs were therefore repeated as heard, unlike those of the Ashkenazi communities, which were translated into Yiddish. For almost four hundred years, until the late 19th century when ethnographers wrote down the verses (in Hebrew script), identical Sephardi songs have been orally transmitted from mother to daughter in communities as far afield as Turkey, Morocco, Bosnia, Greece, and Holland. Because it is an oral tradition, textual variations occur, with adaptations that may include Jewish references. Rather more remarkable is the number of texts that remain unchanged, sung to identical melodies common amongst the widely spread Sephardi communities, and indicating extraordinary tenacity in identifying with a culture from which the Jews suffered persecution and ultimate expulsion. The essentialist element in the Sephardi domestic canon of song lies both in melody and language. Thus in her version of one of the best known songs of the repertoire, *Durme Durme*, Flory Jagoda, who

[19] See Ruth Gay, *The Jews of Germany* (New Haven and London: Yale University Press, 1992), 72–80. Also, Devra Kaye, *Seyder Tkhines: The Forgotten Book of Common Prayer for Jewish Women* (Philadelphia: The Jewish Publication Society, 2004).

[20] For references to research into the history of the language of Portuguese Jewry and its absence from the Sephardi corpus of domestic song see www.jewish-languages.org/judeo-portuguese.html

now lives in California but who was born in Sarajevo, demonstrates that the song is a Jewish lullaby.[21]

Durme durme izhiko de Madre	Sleep, sleep, Mother's little boy
Durme durme sin ansia dolor	*Sleep free from worry and pain*
Sienti joya palavrikas de tu Madre	*Listen, my joy, to your Mother's words*
Las palavras di Shema Yisrael	*The words of the Shema Yisrael*
Durme durme izhiko de Madre	Sleep, Mother's little boy
Con ermozura de Shema Yisrael	With the beauty of the *Shema Yisrael*

However, apart from the two references to the *Shema* which puts the lullaby firmly into the context of Jewish night prayer, the language remains essentially that of medieval Castillian.

The text is, however, a version of a song that has no Jewish allusions and is demonstrably an adult love-song. The performer, Judy Frankel, describes the song as taught to her by two Sephardi women, Selma Mizrachi and Sara Levi, who both hail from the Greek island of Rhodes.[22] The melody is identical to that sung by Jagody, and whilst the language remains Castillian Spanish, the absence of anything Jewish in the text suggests that this is the original song on which Jagoda's text is based. In this version the lyrics describe a rather dark song of unrequited love.

Durme, durme	Sleep, sleep
Mi alma donzella	*My beautiful damsel.*
Durme, durme	Sleep, sleep
Sin ansia y dolor.	Wit*hout worry or sorrow.*
Heq tu sclavo tanto dezea	Here is your slave who only wishes
Ver tu sueño con grande amor	To watch over your sleep with the greatest of love
Ver tu sueño con grande amor.	To watch over your sleep with the greatest of love.
Hay dos años que sufre mi alma	For two years my soul has been suffering
Por ti, joya, mi Linda dama	For you, my jewel, my lovely lady
Por ti, joya, mi Linda dama.	For you, my jewel, my lovely lady.
Siente, siente al son de mi guitarra	Listen, listen to the sound of my guitar
Siente, hermosa, mis males cantar	Listen my lovely to my sad song
Siente, hermosa, mis males cantar.	Listen my lovely to my sad song.[23]

By adhering in this extraordinary way to the songs of medieval Spain, the dispersed Sephardi have inevitably become custodians of a body of songs that might otherwise have been lost. Thus, anyone wishing to investigate the folk music of medieval Spain is encouraged to visit the canon of Sephardi women's music as a primary source, creating a 21st Century position in which medieval Castillian folk music goes under the rubric of the Sephardi tradition. This open acknowledgement of Jewish ownership of melody and text that was originally Spanish would seem the result of four hundred years of careful preservation that might not have existed had not the Jews of the Iberian peninsula been expelled from their homes. Attempts by expatriate groups to preserve their culture are regularly documented, but what is

---

[21] For Jagody's *Durme, Durme* see *Kantikas di Mi Nona (Songs of my Grandmother)* Audio CD, Global Village B00003A9PO (30 April 1996).

[22] Judy Frankel, *Stairway of Gold: Songs of the Sephardim,* Audio CD, Global Video B00008GQ12 (19 October 1995).

[23] Translation taken from liner notes for Frankel Audio CD (1995).

remarkable in this instance is that the texts and melodies that remained so similar were orally transmitted in diverse communities throughout Europe and North Africa.

Conclusion

The examples of Hasidic *nigun* appear to demonstrate that Hasidic philosophy attaches considerable significance to music whilst at the same time allowing that the sanctity assigned to a melody lies in its use rather than itself. In the main, once a melody is adopted as a spiritual vehicle it becomes elevated and may not be relegated to its former status, although there are examples where the origins are recognized and recorded. In the unusual case of the Lubavitch adoption of the *Marseillaise*, the group goes further in its belief that the melody's application as a *nigun* has a mystical effect on its reception as a national anthem. In this instance the sanctity attached to the music's acquired status influences its reception in its original role.

Within the rather different area of folk melody, the example of Sephardi women's song presents a case of musical adoption and maintenance which would seem to indicate the group's desire to sustain the memory of previous cultural integration. By their act of preservation, the women of the dispersed Sephardi communities became the custodians of a medieval Iberian folk tradition and language that was dissipated by natural evolution within Spain. By tenaciously retaining the medieval songs and ballads, the dispersed communities appear to have authentically reproduced the medieval songs of Castillian Spain, since the widely placed communities continue to sing near identical text to identical melody. However, rather than described as custodians of a Spanish tradition, Sephardi women are regarded as possessors of their own essential recognizable body of folk-song convention. Thus the Hasidic and the Sephardi paradigms identify processes by which music, although initially adopted, has become identifiably theirs.

BIBLIOGRAPHY

Adorno, Theodor, *Beethoven: The Philosophy of Music* (Palo Alto, Stanford University Press, 1997).

Braun, Joachim, *Music in Ancient Israel/Palestine: Archeological, Written and Comparative Sources* (Grand Rapids, Michigan: Eerdmans Publications, 2002).

Gay, Ruth, *The Jews of Germany* (New Haven and London: Yale University Press, 1992).

Idelsohn, Abraham Zvi, *Jewish Music: Its Historical Development* (New York: Schocken Books, 1967).

Kaye, Devra, *Seyder Tkhines: The Forgotten Book of Common Prayer for Jewish Women* (Philadelphia: The Jewish Publication Society, 2004).

Kilmer, Anne, 'The Discovery of an Ancient Theory of Mesopotamian Music', *Proceedings of the American Philosophical Society* (1971).

Lipsker, Eli, and Velvel Pasternak, *Chabad Melodies: Songs of the Lubavitcher Chassidim* (Baltimore: Tara Publications, 1997).

'Mi Sinai Niggunim', *Encyclopedia Judaica* (Israel: CD Rom Edition, Israel: Judaica Multimedia Ltd., 1997).

Sacks, Oliver, *Musicophilia* (New York, Alfred A. Knopf, 2007).

Vinaver, Chemjo, *Anthology of Hassidic Music* (Jerusalem: Hebrew University of Jerusalem, 1985).

Zalmanoff, Samuel, *Sefer Hanigunim*, 2 vols (Brooklyn: Nichoach, no date).

Web-Sites

www.jewish-languages.org/judeo-portuguese.html

Personal Communication

French Ministry of Culture Official. *Personal telephone communication with this author* (3 May 2000).

Sperber, S. *Personal communication with this author* (1961).

Discography

Frankel, Judy, *Stairway of Gold: Songs of the Sephardim*, Audio CD, Global Video B00008GQ12 (19 October 1995).

Jagoda, Flory, *Kantikas Di Mi Nona*, Audio CD, Global Village B00003A0PO (30 April 1996).

Nigunei Satmar 5733. Audio Cassette, CDD #103 (no further attribution).

Yidel Werzberger, *Nigunei Yomim Noroyim.* Audio Cassette (New York: 5735 Autumn 2004).

The Rebbe's Nigunim. Audio Cassette (New York: Y&M Music Productions, 1995).

ARE HOLOCAUST VICTIMS JEWISH? LOOKING AT PHOTOGRAPHS IN THE IMPERIAL WAR MUSEUM HOLOCAUST EXHIBITION

K. Hannah Holtschneider*

This essay argues that the representation of Jewish identifications in the permanent Holocaust exhibition in the Imperial War Museum, London, tries to balance the self-representation of Jewish victims with the demands of a perpetrator-led narrative that by necessity characterises Jews in antisemitic terms. The analysis is based on close readings of the exhibition, in particular of the photographic displays, archival sources and interviews with curators. Ultimately, the exhibition is unable to represent Jewish victims of the Holocaust as subjects with agency, because it focuses on the process of destruction at the expense of expounding on what was destroyed. This may be inevitable in a Holocaust exhibition. Nonetheless, the article poses the question whether such an approach has the consequence of unwittingly perpetuating antisemitic representations of Jews and Jewishness.

The Holocaust exhibition at the Imperial War Museum, London (IWM), opened to the public in the summer of 2000, proclaims in its statement of purpose that it understands the Holocaust primarily as the genocide of European Jews, though the fact that the Nazis also persecuted and murdered millions of non-Jews, albeit in arguably less systematic ways, is referenced. This is the wording opening the permanent Holocaust exhibition at the IWM:

> Under the cover of the Second World War, for the sake of their 'New Order', the Nazis sought to destroy all the Jews of Europe. For the first time in history, industrial methods were used for the mass extermination of a whole people. Six million people were murdered, including 1,500,000 children. This event is called the Holocaust. The Nazis enslaved and murdered millions of others as well. Gypsies, people with physical and mental disabilities, Poles, Soviet prisoners of war, trade unionists, political opponents, prisoners of conscience, homosexuals, and others were killed in vast numbers. This exhibition looks at how and why these things happened. (IWM January 2008)

Since the Holocaust is seen chiefly as the exclusion, persecution and murder of Jews, I am interested to understand how the exhibition communicates who 'Jews' are in the conceptualisation of the IWM. The analysis is concerned with the IWM's interpretation of what is 'Jewish', that is, the complex nexus of ethnicity, culture, religion, language which articulates people's identifications and belonging, both as they see themselves and as they are seen by others. The representations of Jewishness offered by the IWM Holocaust exhibition need to establish for visitors who the victims of the Holocaust were. To do so, the exhibition employs visual and textual clues which link with the visitors' image of Jews. Only then can the exhibition hope to facilitate learning about the people who became victims, confirming, challenging and/or subverting preconceptions visitors may hold about Jews. What is

---

* Senior Lecturer in Jewish Studies, School of Divinity, University of Edinburgh. Email: H.Holtschneider@ ed.ac.uk

imagined to be 'normatively' Jewish and thus recognisably such for the visitor, is therefore a question guiding the explorations in this paper. I will explore the techniques the museum uses to establish the ethnic and/or cultural identity of the Jewish victims through an analysis of photographic displays in the IWM Holocaust exhibition.

Before we turn to an analysis of photographic displays, we need briefly to examine the relationship of photography to the events of the Holocaust and how this may have a bearing on the 'musealisation' of the Holocaust.

Photography and the Holocaust

World War II quickly became the most photographed battleground to date, photography not only being used officially to document or by journalists to report, but increasingly by individual soldiers who recorded 'their war' on personal hand-held cameras, widely available and affordable by the late 1930s. Merchandise allowing the collection and display of 'my war' became even more popular than during World War I, with soldiers swapping and selling photos with their comrades and sending them home as postcards which reported their news from the battlefield.

Professional photographers in the *Propagandakompanie* (*PK*) took pictures mainly of Eastern European Jews during the war and published these in magazines such as the *Berliner Illustrirte*. These photo essays were conceptualised and arranged in such a way that they clearly exhibit aspects of Nazi antisemitism and make ideological statements about the status of Jews in Nazi thinking.[1] Soldiers of the *Wehrmacht* as well as members of the SS and *Einsatzgruppen* who were keen amateur photographers took their cues from these papers and imitated the style and perspective exhibited there by professionals serving the ends of the party and the government.[2]

The Holocaust was photographed, despite prohibitions against private individuals doing so. Members of the *Propagandakompanie*, employed specifically to record photographic evidence of the destruction of the Jewish enemy, needed the co-operation of the squads of soldiers they worked with. One way to ensure co-operation was the trading of images produced by the professional photographers with the soldiers they accompanied on their murderous missions. Another was the developing and printing of photographs taken by the soldiers themselves. Both activities defied the prohibition on taking photographs, but it was this which led to the widespread availability of images of atrocity involving German soldiers from the *Wehrmacht*, SS and *Einsatzgruppen*. These photographs constitute a significant part of the material evidence of the genocide, in particular in terms of representations of its victims whose lives were so thoroughly destroyed that material objects speaking to their lives are largely lacking. However, their emplotment in Holocaust exhibitions, as we will see, is not uncontested.[3]

---

[1] Loewy, Hanno, ' "… without Masks": Jews through the Lens Of "German Photography" 1933–1945' In *German Photography 1870–1970: Power of a Medium*, eds., Klaus Honnef, Rolf Sachsse, and Karin Thomas (Köln DuMont Buchverlag, 1997), 111.

[2] Loewy, ' "without Masks" ' in Honnef, Sachsse, and Thomas, eds., *German Photography 1870–1970*, 106f.

[3] The visual representation of the Holocaust continues to be a contested field. A concern permeating much writing on the representation of the Holocaust is the notion of its 'unrepresentability'. The present context does not allow (nor call for) an exploration of the debate about possibilities and limitations to the visual representation of the

The curators of the IWM exhibition are trained historians.[4] A design company provided the plans for the use of the layout of the available exhibition space and worked with the curators to translate the historical narrative provided into an exhibition with a clear pathway and carefully composed displays. To understand the use of photographs of victims in the IWM exhibition, it is necessary briefly to consider the functions of photos in historical research.

Historians work with the indexicality of the photograph, that is, they use images to look for signs of a past reality. Photographs are ambiguous historical documents or sources and have only recently begun to receive serious attention from historians as sources/documents in their own right. A prominent reason for this difficult status is the fact that they can be infinitely reproduced – raising questions about what constitutes an original – and a second reason is the fact that they can be manipulated. In common with other historical documents photographs always embody a point of view, they have an author and a perspective. They are interpretations of a reality which was different before the shutter came down and which changed immediately after that moment. Photographs are often viewed as direct references to a past reality, as if seeing an image gives access to what is pictured in an unmediated way. And yet, we know that photographs can be manipulated and that this has been done since the inception of the technique which fixes images on paper. Indeed, that a photograph can be altered was (and is) an attraction, the fact that we can make ourselves look more beautiful than we seem in reality through a few simple changes to an image always was a powerful aspect of photography, well before the invention of photoshop. Photographs are not neutral, they are not a straightforward reproduction of reality.

If photographs are understood as interpretations of reality, what matters to a historian is not only a consideration of the technology and technique of producing particular images and the relation of the subject that has thus been rendered visible, but also the history of a photograph's reproduction, distribution and display. Connected to this are questions regarding the meaning assigned to a photograph. Meanings are created through the relationship between the viewer and the image. This relationship undergoes changes from the moment the shutter is pressed. The interpretation of the scene through the viewfinder is different from the meaning the photograph has to its author on first viewing it on paper. And the meaning shifts again at subsequent viewings. Different meanings are assigned by other people who view the image in a variety of contexts. For example, a portrait of a soldier in the battlefield can be used as a documentation of 'I was here'; it can be seen as an evocation of his presence in the home of his family who received that image from the battlefield; it

---

Holocaust. The Holocaust is subject of major exhibition projects which prove popular with the general public and have become important educational tools, and as such *is* represented with the help of visual media. Only the method and a/effects of one aspect of a specific example of the musealisation of the Holocaust are the topic of this paper.

[4] The Holocaust Exhibition Project Team at the IWM continues to be led by historian Suzanne Bardgett. By contrast, the United States Holocaust Memorial Museum's exhibition was put together under the leadership of Shaike Weinberg, whose background was in theatre and performance and who had previously curated the exhibition at Tel Aviv's Diaspora Museum, Bet Hatefutsoth. This latter exhibition pioneered the approach of 'a museum without objects', configuring a museum as 'story telling in a three-dimensional space' which relies on the visitor's total immersion with all senses in the exhibition narrative. Using simulation techniques, Weinberg stressed the performative aspect of a museum, treating the exhibition as a '*Gesamtkunstwerk*' that has to be experienced in its totality, thus decidedly moving away from traditional exhibition strategies of carefully arranged showcases with labelled objects.

could commemorate his life if he was killed in action; it can forge a relation to a different period of history if viewed today, acting as a springboard for imagining a historically distant life which looks deceptively close due to the lifelike features of a photograph. While the actual image does not change, its uses do and thereby its meaning. Looking at historical photographs today means that we are often looking at people who were dead before we were born and their photographs relate a moment which has been and gone and which we are only able to read with the knowledge that that person is no more, or who, if they are still alive, may no longer bear much physical resemblance to the person represented.

Exhibiting the Holocaust

History museums and exhibitions split into different genres of exhibiting the past. Traditional exhibitions show objects of historical interest assembled, categorised and labelled, and leave the visitor to chart their own path through the exhibition area. Current preference in the design of Holocaust exhibitions favours *narrative* and *memorial* exhibitions, each making slightly different demands on the visitor. [5]

Narrative exhibitions lead the visitor through a historical topic mostly in a linear fashion, so that competing interpretations of the historical evidence are often obliterated in favour of the presentation of one authoritative master narrative. The visitor has hardly any opportunity to deviate from the path of the exhibition and the dominant narrative seeks to provide the audience with a self-contained and accessible story. Many such exhibitions are object-led in the sense that historical artefacts are presented as access points to an experience of the past. Some exhibitions also work with emotive devices such as walk-in recreations of historical spaces, puppets, or sounds and smells to enable the visitor to experience an illusion of the past. In this respect historical exhibitions compete with the heritage industry which employs similar strategies to create 'experiences of history' in actual historical settings or in recreations of historical environments. [6]

Memorial museums not only endeavour to provide a historical narrative, but also enable the commemoration of historical events and people by those most closely connected to the subject of the exhibition. Thus memorial museums aim at two different audiences: at those who seek commemoration and at those who seek education about the history in question. The educational aspects of such exhibitions are akin to the strategies employed by narrative museums, while the architectural surroundings and the placement of artefacts serve as spaces and guides for commemoration. [7]

---

[5] A leading example for a *narrative* and *memorial* exhibition is the USHMM. For the following see Katrin Pieper, *Musealisierung des Holocaust: Das Jüdische Museum Berlin und das U.S. Holocaust Memorial Museum in Washington D.C. Ein Vergleich* (Köln: Böhlau Verlag, 2006), 29f.

[6] Stephen Greenberg, 'The Vital Museum' in Suzanne MacLeod, ed., *Reshaping Museum Space: Architecture, Design, Exhibition, Museum Meanings* (London: Routledge, 2005), 230–233.

[7] For example, the USHMM seeks to achieve an authoritative narration of the history of the Holocaust and at the same time serves as a space for commemoration of the victims of the Holocaust by individuals and groups. The USHMM has some spaces dedicated specifically to memorialisation. One might argue that the entire museum is a commemorative space and that all objects displayed therein can be invested with commemorative value. Cf. Oren Baruch Stier, *Committed to Memory: Cultural Mediations of the Holocaust* (Amherst, MA: University of Massachusetts Press, 2003); Andrea Liss, *Trespassing through Shadows: Memory, Photography, and the Holocaust* (Minneapolis, MN University of Minnesota Press, 1998).

Holocaust museums and exhibitions share in both strategies of musealising historical topics, though the aspects which invite visitors to imagine themselves as part of the narrative exhibited are carefully limited so as not to offer a chamber of horrors or to violate the memory of the victims. The latter is an important aspect of debates surrounding exhibits, such as what can be displayed and how. Holocaust exhibitions are universally constructed with educational objectives which aim to provide learning opportunities relevant to the context of the visitors' lives, while informing visitors about the history of the genocide of European Jews. Thus visitors are supposed to connect the narrative of the exclusion, persecution and murder of Jews with current social-political debates about xenophobia, immigration and racism. The exhibitions themselves may not necessarily make those connections explicitly (though some do, for example Museum of Tolerance - Beith Hashoah, Anne Frank House Amsterdam). However, educational materials aimed at teenage visitors (often as part of organised school visits) suggest that learning about the Holocaust offers lessons which can be applied to the immediate context of the teenagers' lives.[8]

In German academia there is a growing body of writing which addresses the question of history teaching in museums. Pedagogical concerns are joined with the craft of the historian and curator to communicate 'history'. In a recent study entitled *Visual History und Geschichtsdidaktik*,[9] Christoph Hamann seeks to do two things: to offer an interpretation or understanding of historically significant photographs and to facilitate an interpretation of reality which takes place through/in photographs, that is, to consider photographs in relation to particular cultures of looking and the gaze as they relate to particular images.

Hamann judges that younger visitors to museum exhibitions are used to much higher levels of regular visual stimulation than previous generations, while also finding that their visual literacy, that is their ability to interpret images, does not seem to have increased to the same degree.[10] This lack of critical viewing ability poses a problem to those interested in teaching history through images, a strategy that Holocaust exhibitions rely on. Rather than giving rise to questions about the historical period that is exhibited, photographs appear to be perceived as visual confirmation of previously held ideas. Hamann thus concludes that photographs are literally 'not seen'.

Hamann's work raises questions with regard to the ability of museum visitors to 'read' photographs critically, and concerns the wider context of the production of exhibitions which rely to a significant extent on photographs to support and convey their narrative. Holocaust exhibitions consider visitor groups who are used to much higher visual stimulation than the curators building the exhibition are used to. Curators often are historians (as in the IWM), whereas professionals trained in museum studies are still too new on the scene to constitute a majority among those conceptualising and researching exhibitions. This is true in regard to the IWM Holocaust exhibition which was curated in the late 1990s, for instance. When we consider this together with the fact that historians until very recently only reluctantly considered photographs as historical sources, we might usefully wonder whether curators actually bring a more developed visual literacy to the exhibitions than their young visitors.

---

[8] The tendency to encourage such connections has been criticised, in particular as it explicitly instrumentalises the Holocaust for contemporary political aims.

[9] Christoph Hamann, *Visual History und Geschichtsdidaktik: Bildkompetenz in der historisch-politischen Bildung*, Geschichtswissenschaft 53 (Herbolzheim: Centaurus Verlag, 2007).

[10] Hamann, *Visual History und Geschichtsdidaktik*), 37f.

Another concern, relating not specifically to the use of photographs but more broadly to the representation of the Holocaust in exhibitions, is raised by Dirk Rupnow. His study *Vernichten und Erinnern* has recently shown in detail that the Nazis' own plans to 'memorialise' Jews were far advanced, not least through archival projects at institutions promoting '*Judenforschung*', whose employees researched and published on Jewish history from an antisemitic perspective, and through planned exhibitions and museums. The best known among these museum projects was the planned Jewish museum in Prague, which was supposed to exhibit the remnants of Jewish culture(s) in Europe, authoritatively emplotted in a Nazi antisemitic narrative.[11] Rupnow studied the ways in which the Nazi government encouraged the collection of Jewish ritual objects, written sources and visual evidence of Jewish life alongside the accumulation of evidence documenting the murder of Jews. '*Judenforschung*' aimed at the preservation of a particular perspective on Jewish history, inscribing an antisemitic 'normativity' in the representation of Jews for the purposes of perpetuating and justifying antisemitism: the photographic evidence of the persecution of Jews and their murder was supposed to illustrate the necessity of the annihilation of Jewish life and culture.

What is significant in relation to my contribution is the challenge Rupnow raises to contemporary musealisations of the Holocaust. He asks whether it is possible that the intricate connections the Nazis drew between their crimes and the history of their victims may have been replicated in contemporary forms of Holocaust remembrance and representation,[12] such that the antisemitic 'normativity' of Nazi representations of Jews can be found in contemporary Holocaust exhibitions. Rupnow hints at this possibility because many Holocaust exhibitions explicitly rely on evidence produced by the vicitimisers to document the process of murder, and because exhibitions often employ a perpetrator-led narrative. The IWM is no exception here. Hence, we may well ask whether it is possible that the IWM exhibition may rely too uncritically on perpetrator evidence to represent the lives and deaths of the victims. With these considerations in mind we now turn to the permanent Holocaust exhibition at the IWM London.

Representations of Jewishness in the IWM Holocaust exhibition

The IWM Holocaust exhibition unfolds in a linear narrative on two floors.[13] The upper floor considers Nazi ideology, discriminatory legislation, intimidation, persecution, emigration and violence, culminating in the move towards murder in the T4 euthanasia programme. Descending to the lower floor, the exhibition continues with the beginning of war, the invasion of the Soviet Union, and the ensuing process of murder through *Einsatzgruppen*, ghettos, *Aktion Reinhard*, Auschwitz-Birkenau, slave labour, rescue and resistance, to the end of the war and war crimes trials. The organisation of the material deliberately allows the perspective of the murderers to guide the visitor through the history of persecution and murder, because this allows the development of a storyline which gives a common purpose

---

[11] Dirk Rupnow, *Vernichten und Erinnern: Spuren Nationalistischer Gedächtnispolitik* (Göttingen: Wallstein, 2005).

[12] Rupnow, *Vernichten und Erinnern*, 339ff.

[13] For a discussion of this presentation strategy which is prevalent in most Holocaust exhibitions cf. Pieper, *Musealisierung des Holocaust*, 29f.

to seemingly disparate events. The narrative is illustrated with artefacts, photographs and testimony from victims. Throughout the exhibition, survivor testimony accompanies the narrative at every stage except in the display on the *Einsatzgruppen* and Jewish resistance. Thus video and audio testimonies from survivors (mostly Jewish) who are today living in Britain describe impressions of pre-war life, the discrimination following the Nuremberg Laws, persecution of Jews in Poland, life in the ghettos, deportation, the murder process and life in Auschwitz-Birkenau, slave labour, liberation and reflections on life after the Holocaust.

Photographs play an important part in this musealisation of the Holocaust, functioning as evidence and illustration. Photo murals dominate entire walls and the background of display cases, setting the tone and creating the atmosphere, communicating that 'this has been'. Photos represent both the victims before they became victims *and* their dehumanisation and murder. According to the curators, photographs are supposed to bring home 'the truth' or 'the reality' of the process of persecution and murder.[14] The vast majority of photographic evidence and images of victims shown in the exhibition was produced by perpetrators. There are images which depict violence which were taken by victims themselves, but these are rare and not always identified as such (an exception are the photographs taken clandestinely and under great danger by the *Sonderkommando* in Birkenau in 1944 and then smuggled out of the camp, which are displayed and discussed on a separate panel).

The IWM does not operate a censorship policy on photographs which are deemed too violent or pornographic, unlike the United States Holocaust Memorial Museum in Washington, DC (USHMM). The IWM curators wished to avoid the 'peep show' effect produced by the screens at the USHMM behind which images too gruesome for open display are visible.[15] Rather, the curators suggest that by the time visitors reach photographs of atrocities such as the humiliation of Jews in Poland, as well as the crimes committed by or alongside the *Einsatzgruppen*, they will have been adequately prepared to be able to cope with images such as those of recently violated women photographed on the streets of Lvov.[16] The curators argue that such images need to be exhibited, because they are witnesses to the reality of the events. At the same time, the curatorial team decided not to include an 'evidence layer' which would have commented on the origins of the objects and photographs in the exhibition, the reason being that visitors should not have to deal with too much text. Limiting text in exhibitions has well-founded museological reasons, since an exhibition is not 'a book on a wall'. An exhibition is supposed to engage various senses and appeal to a variety of audiences whose literacy levels differ. Hence the use of space, the placement of objects, images and text in relation to each other is what creates an 'exhibition experience', something that would be lost if visiting an exhibition is akin to reading a book. However, the curators argue that the history of the Holocaust needs to be displayed in an authoritative linear narrative, so that the visitor is able to learn exactly that which the curators wish to impart. They reject the option that this exhibition should offer opportunities to reflect critically on

---

[14] Interview with Suzanne Bardgett, IWM Holocaust Exhibition Project Director, 1 July 2008; interview with James Taylor and Paul Salmons, IWM, 4 July 2008.

[15] Interview with James Taylor and Paul Salmons, IWM, 4 July 2008.

[16] Thus the extremely shocking and challenging quality of evidence of the Holocaust is contained so the exhibition narrative can be assimilated without traumatising the visitors. Cf. Stephen Greenberg, 'The Vital Museum' in Suzanne MacLeod, ed., *Reshaping Museum Space: Architecture, Design, Exhibition, Museum Meanings* (London: Routledge, 2005), 232f.

the practice of curators, because the exhibition is about the Holocaust and not about museology. They also reject the organisation of the exhibition narrative in a less linear fashion which would allow visitors to explore specific geographical perspectives on the Holocaust and thus reflect on various ways of perceiving, interpreting, learning about and emplotting the events which are today summarised under the label 'Holocaust'.[17]

With this general characterisation of the IWM Holocaust exhibition in mind we now turn to the question central to this paper which was prompted by the observation that the IWM defines the Holocaust chiefly as the exclusion, persecution and murder of Jews. I am seeking to understand how the exhibition communicates who 'Jews' are and what is 'Jewish' in the IWM's interpretation of the victims' culture(s) and lives. As argued at the outset, the representations of Jewishness offered by the IWM Holocaust exhibition need to connect with the visitors' image of Jews to be able to facilitate learning about the people who became victims, confirming, challenging and/or subverting preconceptions visitors may hold about Jews. What is imagined to be a 'normative' expression of Jewish identity is therefore worth asking when examining the techniques the museum uses to establish the ethnic and/or cultural identity of victims who are central to the exhibition narrative.

Photographs and Jewishness

How, then, does the visitor learn about the Jewishness of the victims?[18] What makes the victims Jewish in the representational strategy of the IWM? The photographs in the opening area of the exhibition are intended to depict 'Life before the Nazis' and are supposed to allow the visitor to gather their thoughts in preparation for the exhibition proper.[19] The display includes pictures of traditional orthodox men and a *bar mitzvah* boy. The silent film playing in this area includes images of Jewish men in traditional Hasidic dress and the video testimony makes references to religious ritual. While not explored at that stage, references to Jewish religious practice are taken up again in the showcase on Jewish life which is surrounded by a display of antisemitic writings and posters and placed in the alcove which explains the history of antisemitism. The alcove also shows a specially produced film which explains in two sections: 'Who are the Jews?' and 'How did antisemitism arise?' The curators wish to make the point that Jewish life always existed alongside antisemitism. And yet, the arrangement may suggest more than that, in particular when the subtle interpretive hint of the placement of artefacts relating to Jewish life on a white background and the display of antisemitic goods on a black background is overlooked. Then the seemingly indiscriminate intermingling of antisemitic works with artefacts of Jewish life suggests that Jewish life should be interpreted with the help of antisemitic works, or the display can be read as Jewish life

---

[17] Interview with Taylor and Salmons, 4 July 2008; cf. also Pieper, *Musealisierung des Holocaust*, 29.

[18] The following discussion excludes the minority of victims who were persecuted as Jews but who did not identify themselves as Jewish.

[19] The Holocaust exhibition differs from the other permanent exhibitions in the IWM which, as the name of the museum already indicates, deal primarily with war from a British perspective. The visitor, who leaves the large open space at the centre of the museum filled with the machinery of war such as tanks and planes of both world wars, and turns to the Holocaust exhibition on the 4th floor, is given a moment of collection and orientation in this foyer to the exhibition proper.

conforming to – or even confirming? – antisemitic views of Jews.[20] Rupnow's question as to whether today's Holocaust exhibitions may unintentionally reproduce Nazi models of representing Jewish history and culture is particularly pertinent here, since the narrative of the IWM exhibition is closely linked to the perspective of the perpetrators and evidence produced by the victimisers.[21]

A dedicated exploration of Jewish culture in Europe before the Holocaust is lacking in the IWM Holocaust exhibition. The minutes of the meetings of the Advisory Group to the Holocaust Exhibition Project Team at the IWM indicate that there were recurrent intense debates on this subject.[22] In particular in the early stages of discussing the translation of the historical narrative into the exhibition design, some members repeatedly voiced the fear that the upper floor of the exhibition lacked a section on Jewish life before the Nazis and 'that there was a danger that the Museum might end up *teaching antisemitism by using material created by the Nazis* and that their distortions would not be conveyed.'[23] The board concluded that 'an ethnographic approach would be out of place',[24] because the subject of the exhibition is the murder of Jews and how the genocide came about, not Jewish history as such. As a result, Jewishness is mainly encountered through artefacts such as an intact Torah scroll in the showcase on Jewish life and antisemitism, a burnt Torah scroll in the *'Kristallnacht'* display, a part of a Torah scroll which was hidden in the Warsaw ghetto and the remains of a Torah scroll found in Hannover in the display about the discovery of the camps by the Allies.

Jewishness is also referenced through photographs of 'recognisably Jewish'[25] Jews – in contrast to assimilated Jews who are visually indistinguishable from their non-Jewish compatriots – a strategy which plays on antisemitic stereotypes and this may compound Nazi antisemitic renditions of Jewish life. The space addressing the ghettos – which concentrates on Warsaw and Lodz – contains a section on 'Spiritual Resistance' which assembles material relating to cultural activities such as theatre performances as well as religious services. Among other items, such as the Torah scroll already mentioned, we find a list of rabbis authorised by the local 'Jewish Council' to perform weddings in the Lodz ghetto, marriage documents and photographs of religious ceremonies such as a wedding and a circumcision. It is not clear who took the photos displayed in this section and who can be seen in these photos. Some photographs which depict the conditions inside ghetto tenements and workshops are likely to be self-portrayals of the ghetto inhabitants, evidently

---

[20] Cf. also Tony Kushner, 'The Holocaust and the Museum World in Britain: A Study of Ethnography' in Sue Vice, ed., *Representing the Holocaust: In Honour of Bryan Burns* (Vallentine Mitchell, London, 2003), 24f; K. Hannah Holtschneider, 'Victims, Perpetrators, Bystanders? Witnessing, Remembering and the Ethics of Representation in Museums of the Holocaust' in *Holocaust Studies* 13:1 (2007), 91f.

[21] It is possible that all attempts to contrast the perpetrator perspective with self-representations of victims are not enough to subvert antisemitic interpretations of Jewish life. For example, in the display about the T4 Euthanasia programme images of children who were subjected to medical experiments are, where available, juxtaposed with family photographs of the same children, in order to challenge the perspective of the images produced by perpetrators (Interview with Taylor and Salmons, 4 July 2008). Such a display strategy is not followed for the representation of Jews, nor would it necessarily always be possible to do so.

[22] Archival materials relating to the creation of the Holocaust exhibition are located in the IWM.

[23] Minutes of the third meeting of the Advisory Group 12 June 1997. The topic was also discussed at the Group's fourth meeting on 20 April 1998 when it was made clear that 'The Museum had decided not to devote a specific section to the subject but was still dealing with it in prominent and easily accessible places'. The topic surfaced again at Group's meeting on 23 April 1999 when the exhibition was already physically under construction.

[24] Minutes of the third meeting of the Advisory Group 12 June 1997.

[25] Minutes of Advisory Group meeting 23 April 1999.

taken with the approval of those pictured. Other photographs show smugglers at work, the photographer having been positioned such that neither the SS nor the smugglers were able to observe the camera. In addition, there are images of street life which have a documentary character and it is difficult to tell who may have taken them. Ghetto inhabitants included professional photographers who continued their work, regularly publishing in ghetto newspapers, documenting the work of the respective ghetto's *Judenrat* and also accumulating a photographic record of their surroundings for themselves.[26] Since the majority of the images in this section are labelled only in order to provide an account of what is visible, but not who took the photo and what we know of the conditions in and the purpose for which the photo was taken, the visitor is left with no help to decipher the photographic illustrations which accompany the narrative of destruction. This display is one of the last opportunities in the exhibition narrative to have photographic evidence of the victims' interpretations of their lives at the time the events were unfolding.

The photos in the ghetto section function as illustrations of the text panel and are not artefacts in their own right, which explains why captions were often deemed unnecessary. This contrasts with the much more detailed depiction of the 'industry of murder', which names responsible individuals (albeit in a token effort) and describes their functions in the murder process. The victims, although identified on video testimony and in display cases addressing the fate of individuals, are almost always representative of 'everyman' or part of an anonymous mass of photographs and not the leaders of communities or individuals who carried responsibility for larger groups of people. To name only a few better known examples, one misses prominent reference to the leaders of Jewish Councils or to leading rabbis, or to the group associated with the historian Emmanuel Ringelblum which gathered evidence of the murder process in the Warsaw ghetto.

Religious Jews were deemed to be 'recognisably Jewish' by the Advisory Group and there the question arises what function is served by displaying 'recognisably Jewish' Jews. One possibility is that it is an acknowledgement that the majority of those who were murdered in the Holocaust came from communities which lived a traditional lifestyle and to whom what we now identify as religiously Jewish dress and comportment was 'normative', everyday, all-encompassing. Or it may be a reflection of the iconic stereotypes of a Jewish 'normativity' which visitors to the exhibition are thought to expect when looking for/at Jews. It appears that those not 'recognisably Jewish' Jews are perceived as 'normal', implicitly suggesting that the visitor has a mental map on which to pinpoint what is 'normal' ('normative'?) in the 1930s in particular in Germany. That which is 'normal' does not seem to need much referencing. Conversely, the 'recognisably Jewish' Jews share the attributes of 'foreign' and 'exotic'. The only resonance in the exhibition for 'foreign' and 'exotic' are antisemitic descriptions of 'the Jew' which characterise the object of their hatred precisely as alien and not belonging, hence needing to be expelled or otherwise gotten rid of.

There are no sections in the exhibition which would introduce the culture which traditional 'recognisably Jewish' people inhabited. The video installations in the entrance cone and in the section on the Warsaw ghetto show scenes of pre-war Jewish life, mainly in *shtetls* in Poland, but these are not commented upon. In these Jewish men in traditional grab are pictured alongside women dressed in the latest fashion, families which include people dressed

---

[26] Cf. for example Janina Struk, *Photographing the Holocaust: Interpretations of the Evidence* (London: I.B. Tauris, 2004).

traditionally and individuals whose clothes are indistinguishable from those of non-Jews. Some survivor testimony demonstrates that many families were divided by their religious observance or lack thereof. And yet, it is difficult, if not impossible, to gather a clearer idea of the religious identifications of Jewish Holocaust victims, in particular notions that go beyond a stereotypical 'normativity'. Such references to 'recognisably Jewish' Jews inscribe at best a stereotypical and at worst an antisemitic 'normativity' in representations of Jews.

It seems that photographs of 'recognisably Jewish' Jews are primarily used to point to a version of 'Jewishness' that is instantly recognisable by visitors and that thereby suggests a certain 'normativity'. To have the effect of recognition, it does not seem to matter to the curators who pressed the shutter on the camera or for which purpose the photographs were produced. Hence, perpetrator evidence is employed to tell the story of the Holocaust without reflection on possible implications of using material of victimiser origin, such as prior ideological uses it may have been put to. The corollary of this use of photographs of religious Jews is a reinforcement of antisemitic perspectives on Jewishness which the exhibition has a hard time undercutting. Because these people themselves are at no point given the voice to speak about their own lives, self-understandings and interpretation of the events that made them into victims, the visitor has to rely on interpreting their Jewishness through the implicit messages embedded in the visual clues given by the exhibition – or bring their own independent knowledge to interpret these images. As a result, the fear of members of the Advisory Group that antisemitic images might come to dominate the exhibition appears to have been realised, despite the significant changes to the displays in response to the designers' first proposal.

As already mentioned, the majority of the photographs displayed in the exhibition were taken by victimisers and even if the curators intend to 'stake a new explanatory context [which] can overcome their original purpose'[27], this, as Paul Williams argues, does not alter the fact that

> for victims, the camera was itself an instrument of humiliation and psychological torture. By displaying their pictures, there is a valid fear that museums might perpetuate this original intent, forcing those pictured to remain in submissive subjugation …[28]

The indiscriminate display of photographs taken by victims of themselves before they became victims, of victims in their situation of being persecuted, and of perpetrators documenting their deeds treats photographs in the same way as the exhibition treats survivor testimony: as illustration, rather than historical evidence in their own right.[29] Many but by no means all images are captioned, and the captions identify photographs mainly in their relation to the theme of the main display, that is, they provide an identification of the location at which they were taken and who or what they show. Captions of photographs (and artefacts) use the smallest font size, thus making them more difficult to read. In addition the visitor can only detect the origins of the photographs through a detailed scrutiny of the camera angle and frame of individual pictures, and can then speculate about the journey of the images until they ended up in this particular exhibition. In view of the sheer amount

[27] Paul Williams, *Memorial Museums: The Global Rush to Commemorate Atrocities* (Oxford: Berg, 2007), 57.

[28] Williams, *Memorial Museums*, 57.

[29] Cf. also Isabel Wollaston, 'Negotiating the Marketplace: The Role(s) of Holocaust Museums Today', in *Journal of Modern Jewish Studies* 4 (2005), 4, 69.

of photographs in the exhibition and their frequent assembly in collages it is unrealistic to expect a visitor to perform such detailed analyses. This approach leaves unexplored the different perspectives the photographers took towards their subjects, as well as the various purposes for taking photos and the co-operation (or lack thereof) of the subjects, aspects of a photograph's origin and history which can yield important historical information and encourage the viewer to reflect on their own relationship to the images.[30]

Photographs in the context of the entire exhibition

In the IWM Holocaust exhibition photographs illustrate, giving a visual context for the textual explanations and the placement of historical artefacts, and photographs create atmosphere and set the tone of the exhibition. At points photographs also authenticate the narrative, saying 'this really happened'. This latter function of photographs is particularly evident when images are used to authenticate original artefacts. For example, the display on the ghettos includes a section on the Warsaw ghetto, part of which focuses on an impressive and gruesome artefact: a cart which transported corpses through the streets of the ghetto. The wall in front of which the restored cart is exhibited is covered with an enlarged photograph of just such a cart in use in the Warsaw ghetto. This linking of image and object points to the authenticity of the artefact: the tangible object *here* in the museum really was *there* in the Warsaw ghetto.[31] This suggests that in some cases neither the photograph nor the historical artefact alone are deemed 'authentic' enough, but need each other in order to establish conclusively that 'this has been'.[32] While objects are trusted to convey a sense of historical reality in the exhibition, photographs do not seem to possess such an aura, possibly because they are used for many different purposes: sometimes as historical evidence, sometimes as background which creates a mood and to reinforce emotional messages. Enlarged photographs are used specifically when the cruelty of the perpetrators and the outrage and shock over their deeds is supposed to be emphasised: for example, the close-up portraits of two young women, who were forcibly sterilised as part of the *Rassehygieneprogramm*, are supposed to lead the viewer to reflect about the character of those responsible, judges and doctors;[33] or the large image on the wall behind a tabletop display case about the mass shootings of Lithuanian Jews, which shows a man kneeling at the edge of a mass grave he presumably helped to dig and a gun pointed at his head by a member of the *Einsatzgruppe*.

Thus, a threefold hierarchy of material in the narrative of the exhibition can be established: at the top sits the historical narrative which occupies the most significant place and is inseparable, secondly, from the historical artefacts employed to support it. Without narrative the artefacts would not be able to 'speak', but without artefacts the narrative would lack authentication. Artefacts of the Holocaust by themselves would not be enough to persuade visitors to spend time in the exhibition. Curators repeatedly point to the fact that

---

[30] Cf. for example Hüppauf, Bernd, 'Emptying the Gaze: Framing Violence through the Viewfinder', *New German Critique* 72 (1997); Koch, Gertrud, *Die Einstellung ist die Einstellung: Visuelle Konstruktionen des Judentums* (Frankfurt am Main: Suhrkamp, 1992).

[31] The connection is made, even though it should be clear to the visitor that the cart on the photographs is probably not identical with the cart on display.

[32] Interview with Suzanne Bardgett, 01 July 2008.

[33] Interview with Bardgett, 01 July 2008.

the historical objects associated with the Holocaust are not spectacular or aesthetically pleasing to look at, and therefore need emplotting in a captivating (linear) narrative to entice the visitor to contemplate for example old shoes or a metal spoon.[34] Thus the artefacts need the narrative and vice versa. In last place, therefore, we find the photographs which are, strictly speaking, not necessary for structuring the exhibition narrative.[35] Photographs do not authenticate the narrative by themselves, they can only second what the artefacts prove, or verify the veracity of artefacts. Photographs, visitors know, can be manipulated – a mistrust that is less frequently associated with artefacts due to the authority held by the museum as a social and cultural institution.[36]

Who are 'Jews' in the IWM Holocaust exhibition?

The IWM Holocaust exhibition seems to oscillate between two conflicting demands. On the one hand, the historical meta-narrative, told from the perspective of the Nazi perpetrators, demands that the victims of the Holocaust are defined, via Nazi racist criteria, as Jews. At the same time, the exhibition tries to subvert antisemitic interpretations of Jewish life and history through video testimony and the presentation of ritual objects which articulate Jewish self-understanding and thus are supposed to clarify for the visitor that Jewish self-understandings did not coincide with Nazi interpretations of 'who is a Jew'.

On the other hand, the exhibition also needs to forge an explicit link with the lives of their visitors who, in the overwhelming majority, are not Jewish and have no close ties to those who were victims of the Holocaust. This is where photographs of Jews who do not look 'recognisably Jewish' are employed. Visitors are supposed to experience that Jews are as 'normal' and 'human' as they are themselves, and therefore the exhibition needs to offer the possibility of identification for visitors in an environment that lacks aesthetic or historically fascinating objects. The IWM curators, following the educational directives of the USHMM, believe that the Holocaust 'yields critical lessons for an investigation of human behaviour … [and] … what it means to be a responsible citizen.'[37] Hence, the exhibition seems to wish to keep the category 'victim' as neutral as possible so that it becomes an approximation of a stereotypical ('normative'?) 'Western European' on which the visitor can inscribe their own circumstances and hopes.[38] Thus, 'Jews' can no longer be employed to represent a specific

---

[34] Interview with Taylor and Salmons, 4 July 2008.

[35] Although at the beginning of the curatorial process the concern was raised that artefacts may be difficult to locate and that the narrative of the history of the Holocaust may have to rely on photographs and film (cf. Suzanne Bardgett, 'Film and the Making of the Imperial War Museum's Holocaust Exhibition' in Toby Haggith and Joanna Newman, eds., *Holocaust and the Moving Image: Representations in Film and Television since 1933* [London: Wallflower, 2005], 20).

[36] When photographs are treated as historical artefacts and exclusive evidence, such as in the *Crimes of the Wehrmacht* exhibition, the discovery that some may have been captioned wrongly may lead to challenging the reliability of the historical claims made by the entire exhibition (cf. for example Christian Hartmann, Johannes Hürter, and Ulrike Jureit, eds., *Verbrechen der Wehrmacht: Bilanz einer Debatte*, Beck'sche Reihe 1632 [München: C.H. Beck, 2005]).

[37] David Cesarani, 'Should Britain Have a National Holocaust Museum?' in *Journal of Holocaust Education* 7:3 (1998), 17-27.

[38] See also Kushner's argument that such an approach to the Holocaust is in continuity with historical American and British liberal perspectives on the genocide of Jews in Europe: Tony Kushner, *The Holocaust and the Liberal Imagination: A Social and Cultural History* (Oxford: Blackwell, 1994).

people with complex and divergent histories and identifications or as members of particular culture(s) and minorities in various European societies. Rather than challenging visitor pre-conceptions of who Jews are, the exhibition creates two versions of Jewish 'normativity', one that relies on antisemitic stereotypes and another which assimilates Jews into a gentile Western secular norm.

As a result the geographical and cultural diversity of those who became victims of the Holocaust is increasingly difficult to represent. The curators rejected a preface to the exhibition which addresses 'the culture(s) that was/were lost' because the IWM does not deal in ethnography. Hence, the visitor without prior knowledge of Jewish history in Europe is left with a very vague idea of the cultural, religious, social and political affiliations and allegiances of the people who were murdered during the Holocaust. The curators rejected arranging the narrative according to the perspectives of various groups of Jewish victims, because this was deemed too parochial and lacking authority and overall clarity. Another reason may be the assumption that the majority of visitors will not view the exhibition more than once. Since the pedagogical aim is to leave every visitor with a clear framework of the 'key events' of the Holocaust, the narrative has to offer a logical sequence of events to aid the establishment of the Holocaust in the visitor's mind as a unified and structured whole.

The intention of the IWM exhibition is to tell the story of destruction and not to talk about what was destroyed. This difference in emphasis alone may account for the dominance of perpetrator images of victims. And as such it may be an inevitable consequence of the construction of the exhibition narrative. Yet, it is important to reflect on possible consequences of this choice of representation for the understanding and interpretations of the Jewishness of the victims of the Holocaust for those who visit the exhibition without extensive prior knowledge of Jewish history, culture and religion. If one consequence is the tacit reinforcement of antisemitic constructions of Jewishness, this arguably is a high price to pay for the adoption of this narrative of Holocaust history. Bluntly put: is antisemitism an acceptable by-product of a clearly structured linear narrative of the Holocaust?

Arguably, then, Holocaust victims in the IWM Holocaust exhibition are Jewish only in the sense in which their Jewishness can be linked a) to the explication of their murder – offering Nazi views of their victims – and b) to the expression of their humanity as equivalent to that of the museum visitors. Both strategies of representing Jewishness obliterate Jewish self-understandings and the complexities of pre-war Jewish culture, albeit, one hopes, unwittingly and without malicious intent.

BIBLIOGRAPHY

Bardgett, Suzanne, 'Film and the Making of the Imperial War Museum's Holocaust Exhibition' in Toby Haggith and Joanna Newman, eds., *Holocaust and the Moving Image: Representations in Film and Television since 1933* (London: Wallflower, 2005), 19–25.

Cesarani, David, 'Should Britain Have a National Holocaust Museum?' *Journal of Holocaust Education* 7:3 (1998), 17–27.

Greenberg, Stephen, 'The Vital Museum' in Suzanne MacLeod, ed., *Reshaping Museum Space: Architecture, Design, Exhibition, Museum Meanings* (London: Routledge, 2005), 226–237.

Hamann, Christoph, *Visual History und Geschichtsdidaktik: Bildkompetenz in der historisch-politischen Bildung*, Geschichtswissenschaft 53 (Herbolzheim: Centaurus Verlag, 2007).

Hartmann, Christian, Johannes Hürter, and Ulrike Jureit, eds., *Verbrechen der Wehrmacht: Bilanz einer Debatte*, Beck'sche Reihe 1632 (München: C.H. Beck, 2005).

Holtschneider, K. Hannah, 'Victims, Perpetrators, Bystanders? Witnessing, Remembering and the Ethics of Representation in Museums of the Holocaust', *Holocaust Studies* 13:1 (2007), 84–104.

Hüppauf, Bernd, 'Emptying the Gaze: Framing Violence through the Viewfinder', *New German Critique* 72 (1997), 3–44.

Koch, Gertrud, *Die Einstellung ist die Einstellung: Visuelle Konstruktionen des Judentums* (Frankfurt am Main: Suhrkamp, 1992).

Kushner, Tony, *The Holocaust and the Liberal Imagination: A Social and Cultural History* (Oxford: Blackwell, 1994).

Kushner, Tony, 'The Holocaust and the Museum World in Britain: A Study of Ethnography' in Sue Vice, ed., *Representing the Holocaust: In Honour of Bryan Burns* (Vallentine Mitchell, London, 2003), 13–40.

Liss, Andrea, *Trespassing through Shadows: Memory, Photography, and the Holocaust* (Minneapolis, MN: University of Minnesota Press, 1998).

Loewy, Hanno, ' "… without Masks": Jews through the Lens of "German Photography" 1933–1945' in Klaus Honnef, Rolf Sachsse, and Karin Thomas, eds., *German Photography 1870–1970: Power of a Medium* (Köln: DuMont Buchverlag, 1997), 100–114.

Pieper, Katrin, *Musealisierung des Holocaust: Das Jüdische Museum Berlin und das U.S. Holocaust Memorial Museum in Washington D.C. Ein Vergleich* (Köln: Böhlau Verlag, 2006).

Rupnow, Dirk, *Vernichten und Erinnern: Spuren nationalsozialistischer Gedächtnispolitik* (Göttingen: Wallstein Verlag, 2005).

Stier, Oren Baruch, *Committed to Memory: Cultural Mediations of the Holocaust* (Amherst, MA: University of Massachusetts Press, 2003).

Struk, Janina, *Photographing the Holocaust: Interpretations of the Evidence* (London: I.B. Tauris, 2004).

Williams, Paul, *Memorial Museums: The Global Rush to Commemorate Atrocities* (Oxford: Berg, 2007).

Wollaston, Isabel, 'Negotiating the Marketplace: The Role(s) of Holocaust Museums Today', *Journal of Modern Jewish Studies* 4 (2005), 63–80.